CONSCIOUSNESS BEYOND DEATH

www.mascotbooks.com

Consciousness Beyond Death:
True Stories of Signs, Messages, and Timing

Second printing. This Mascot Books edition printed in 2023.

The author has tried to recreate events, locales, and conversations from her memories of them. In order to maintain their anonymity, in some instances the author may have changed the names of individuals and places, or identifying characteristics and details such as physical properties, occupations, and places of residence. The views and opinions expressed in this book are solely those of the author. These views and opinions do not necessarily represent those of the publisher or staff.

Cover design by Abigail Freed
Author photo by Bridgett Woody

For more information, please contact:
Mascot Books, an imprint of Amplify Publishing Group
620 Herndon Parkway, Suite 220
Herndon, VA 20170
info@mascotbooks.com

Library of Congress Control Number: 2022917054
CPSIA Code: PRV0723B
ISBN-13: 978-1-63755-518-7

Printed in the United States

To those who have left before me
(you know who you are):
thank you for your continued support!

Consciousness Beyond Death

True Stories of Signs, Messages, and Timing

SOPHIA DEMAS

CONTENTS

FOREWORD

DEBRA GREENE, PHD

This book is an invitation to pay attention to subtle but important cues that can provide ways for you to connect with loved ones who have passed over the threshold. Such communication experienced by Sophia and her close friends directly challenges the accepted notion that consciousness is a product of your brain, and that when your brain dies so does your consciousness.

A book like this, not that many years ago, would have struggled to find an audience. Thankfully times have changed, and science has too, so that the topic of consciousness beyond death is not some far flung, woo-woo notion. Instead, it is a topic taken seriously by adept researchers and supported by an emerging discipline.

The wonderous world of quantum physics seems to be pointing the way. This is a world where particles exist both as distinct particles and spread-out waves at the same time; where particles can spin in two different directions at the same time; where patterns emerge among discrete entities that are not in physical contact; where so-called virtual particles appear and disappear all the time in empty space; where the building blocks of reality exist in a state of potentiality until we observe them; and where particles couple, spin together, "remember" each other, and stay connected forever more at infinite distances from each other! It is in this realm where communication involving signs, messages, and synchronous timing with departed loved ones can occur.

Could it be that an invisible force, outside the realm of established physics, is at play? Could it be that invisible force is consciousness itself, a force that has been disallowed in conventional science since its inception? The amazing stories presented herein answer with a resounding yes!

Research on near death experiences (NDEs) provides some of the most compelling evidence of the primacy of consciousness. These are instances in which a person is clinically brain-dead but continues to have conscious experiences that they report on after "coming back from the dead." If consciousness is a product of the brain, it should die when the brain dies—but it does not. The "conscious but clinically brain-dead" experiences are more widespread than previously thought. In some instances research indicates that up to 25% of the people who "come back" have had these types of experiences.

A full 60-70% of adults in the U.S. believe they will survive after their physical body dies. Although the notion of life after death is central to many religions, the strict dogma and external authority espoused by most religions is giving way and being replaced by spiritual adepts who do not identify with organized religion. These are people who have their own personal relationship with the Divine. They tend to live mindfully, according to inner authority, and establish robust connections with elements of the unseen world.

Experiences involving accurate information received from "guides," profound intuitive insights, and psychic phenomena such as remote viewing, precognition, telepathy, and the like, are not unusual. Researchers who study such phenomena are increasingly convinced that these experiences are expressions of the same thing. Could that "thing" be consciousness itself?

I would say an emphatic yes to the notion that consciousness survives physical death. That consciousness constitutes a powerful, dynamic field of all awareness in which we each participate and that we can tap into at will. This accounts for much of what is referred to as psychic phenomena. Consciousness appears to be a two-way energy/information field that we partake of and participate in co-creating. As such, consciousness is inherently unifying.

Further, it appears that consciousness permeates the universe. If we strip away our tendency to anthropomorphize, to attribute human qualities to this force, consciousness could become the new god-term: More inclusive, less divisive, and backed by science. This is what inspired me to coin the term consciousnist, a term I readily use when asked about my religion.

This book is an engaging contribution to our growing understanding of consciousness. As you read it I invite you to allow yourself to pause, take in, and absorb the essence of each vignette. Sophia is a gifted and trustworthy story teller. The stories are varied and speak for themselves, each one in its own language. Together they create a mosaic of colorful experiences that point to an uplifting conclusion: We may shed our body when we die but our consciousness remains intact, thus we can continue to stay connected with, and benefit from, those who have crossed over. May this book inspire you to expand your awareness and begin to consciously communicate in such ways.

Debra Greene, PhD, author of *Endless Energy*, speaker, and teacher is the founder of Inner Clarity, a consciousness-based modality that gets to the core of energy imbalances and facilitates lasting transformation.

INTRODUCTION

It wasn't until the last moments of my mother's life that I became aware that our time on this earth is just a short break from eternally being one with God/Divine Consciousness. Not that God abandons us when we are born—we enter this world connected to this Universal Consciousness. The human experience, however, is so distracting that we soon begin to forget our union with God.

Research supports what many psychologists claim: that children are born with a natural spiritual compass. *Little*

Big Minds, a book by Marietta McCarty, describes children as natural philosophers and produces evidence that they can grapple with life's "big questions" regarding peace, truth, life, and death. Dr. Robert Coles, a trained pediatric physician and psychiatrist, devoted most of his career to talking with children and listening to them talk about God. He concluded that we can learn much from them. In her book *The Spiritual Child: The New Science on Parenting for Health and Lifelong Thriving*, Dr. Lisa Miller, a psychology professor at Columbia University, proves that by nourishing children's natural spirituality, regardless of the parents' denomination or tradition, they are happier and more resilient. Parents who are nonbelievers can promote this by meditating as a family, fostering compassion, and having weekly gratitude ceremonies. Children who are spiritually supported grow up feeling grateful for their blessings and view obstacles as opportunities for growth. Miller maintains that without this reinforcement innate spirituality drifts away, and a child is left to navigate in a world where addiction is rampant and value is placed mostly on materialism and achievement, resulting in unhealthy competition.

At the end-of-life part of the spectrum, results of numerous studies show that the stronger a person's spiritual discipline, the more likely they are to accept death and await it with peace, even joy. My mother was deeply religious. Two months before her transition, she had withdrawn and her sleeping time had increased. At one point, she was sitting in a chair, awake but with her eyes closed. I asked her what she was thinking. She did not respond. After I told her that she would feel better if she expressed what she was feeling, she opened her eyes and looked into mine. With an angelic look on her face, she said wistfully, "I'm waiting for God to invite me to His house."

I am not claiming to be an expert on death, and this book is not about how spirituality mitigates death anxiety. After compiling coincidences and miracles I had experienced for my memoir *The Divine Language of Coincidence*, I found that there were too many of these events to cram into one book. I began plucking out events that thematically had to do with death. Some may be viewed as simple coincidences, but for me it is without question that through signs, messages, and timing, my departed friends and family members were communicating with me. Most of the incidents happened just after I had thought of the person, asked for their intercession, or wished for their advice.

Many people report receiving timely signs from loved ones who have died. Perhaps, while you're thinking of your father, a cardinal—his favorite bird—flies onto a railing and fixedly stares at you. You smile as you feel his presence.

Or it's your birthday, and after recalling something your grandmother said to you and missing her, you come home to find a bouquet of pink roses, her most beloved flowers, anonymously left on the doorstep, and you interpret it as a sign from her. When someone who has died is in your thoughts and you receive a sign, perfectly timed, you are communicating with them. If you come upon a thing/song/poem that is associated with your loved ones, and it brings them to mind, they are communicating with you. Either way, you have been blessed. I want to be clear and in no way imply that one must be spiritual or religious to receive signs and messages. For example, a friend of mine who is an academic and staunch atheist has maintained with absolute certainty that she heard her father call out her name. It was at the exact moment he was killed in an automobile accident.

The communications that I have been privy to and write about in this book have all contributed to my own spiritual development. I have also included three experiences that happened to close friends, and these also have enriched my journey.

Although I admit that I've received more than my fair share of signs and messages from beyond, I am debunking the response I continually hear from people after telling them of my latest experience: "These things only happen to you." This is far from true. These things happen all the time, and you can realize them, too, if you pay attention. Being present in the moment—conscious awareness—is the only requirement needed to recognize them. To those who believe that consciousness and self-awareness cease to exist after death, I ask: How can communications like the ones that you are about to read possibly happen *without* consciousness?

1

MY FATHER

AN URGE

It tormented me to call home and hear my father in the background moaning in pain. His prostate cancer reoccurrence had been misdiagnosed as rheumatoid arthritis. By the time the cancer was discovered, it had metastasized to his bones. He was ninety-two, and my mother, his sole caregiver, was seventy-three. They still lived in the home where I grew up in Portland, Oregon, and I was working at a Philadelphia architectural firm. I simply could not deal with what was happening. At the time, the road to my spiritual development was more like a barely defined footpath—I was still an endorser of capital punishment.

One Thursday afternoon, I was sitting at my desk, thinking of my father, when I felt an undeniable urge to be with him. I called the airlines and booked the next flight to Portland, leaving for the airport directly from work with just the clothes on my back. I arrived at my parents' house, which I still called home, to find my father in and out of lucidity because of the morphine medication he was taking. Next to his pillow was his wallet with hundred-dollar bills that my mother had placed there to calm his irrational fear of poverty. I spent four days sitting next to his bed, talking with him when he was awake. He would relive the financial hardship that he, his mother, and siblings had endured in a dirt-poor village in Greece. He talked about coming to America alone through Ellis Island when he was fifteen years old, pretending to be eighteen, the cutoff age allowed to enter without a guardian, and how he had spent his youth doing grueling work and sending money back home. He marveled at how he had achieved the American dream and how his success in the stock market allowed him "to make money while I sleep." I had heard the stories countless times before.

On the last day of my visit, as he was coming out of a stupor, my father suddenly grabbed his wallet, fished out a hundred-dollar bill, and handed it to me. I took it because I knew this was the last gift he would ever give me. Then, just as abruptly, he became his old self. “Where did I go wrong with you two kids?” he wondered out loud. “You should be where George [my younger brother] is, married with three kids, and he should be where you are, single with a good job!” My father had not gotten over that I wasn’t married.

Stunned, I reacted with equal fervor. “Fine, Daddy. I’ll just walk up and down the street, carrying a sign that says ‘Husband wanted’ just to make you happy!”

Clearly disturbed, my father leaned forward. Waving his hands back and forth, he said, “No, Dolly [something he had not called me since I was little], I want for you whatever makes you happy!” I hugged him as tightly as I could. My father had just freed me from any future guilt. Once again, my inner voice had guided me well, bringing me to him before returning to Philadelphia to receive his blessing to live my life for myself. He died the following month. Eleven years later, I bought my fiancé’s hundred-dollar wedding band with the bill my father had given me on the last day I was with him.

THE NICKELS

Beginning around eight months after his death, I began to feel that my father was messaging me. First, my mother reported that, upon waking one morning, she had felt my father's hand clasping hers for a solid minute, then letting it go. Strangely, I accepted this as perfectly normal. A short time later, I found a nickel on the street. When I was little, my father would reward me with a nickel for a deed well done. I felt the same surge of joy that I had felt as a child. The nickels kept coming. On one birthday, I was having lunch with a friend at an outside table. As he got up to go inside for a coffee refill, I started thinking of my father. I glanced down at the sidewalk, and there was a nickel. I just knew that wherever he was, he had my back. The night before my birthday, as I was falling asleep, missing him, I asked my father for a sign to let me know that he was with me. I woke up the next morning, feeling something pressing against my cheek. Lifting my head from the pillow, I looked down, and there was a nickel. I toss and turn in my sleep, continually flopping my pillow. How could a nickel survive that and be right under my cheek? I looked to see if there was a wallet or purse nearby from where it could have fallen out, but I found nothing. I knew for sure that the nickel was a birthday kiss from my father.

One day while taking a walk, I realized that I hadn't found a nickel for some time. I asked my father for one, and instantly a message clear as day sounded in my head, "No, I get to give you a nickel when I want to." The next morning, as I opened the gate of the wrought-iron fence onto the brick sidewalk, right there in front of my foot was a gleaming nickel. The nickels continue to come to this day.

THE BEDROOM DOOR

My friend Peg and I were having drinks at a happy hour. Peg was conservative and married to a very wealthy man. I found her husband and his rich white friends to come off as racists. Peg wanted to fix me up with one of them, but I kept dodging the idea. At the time, I was seeing a Black man whom Peg did not approve of. She was drinking two martinis to my one, and as the evening progressed, she became more vociferous with her opinions. I told her I had nothing in common with the guy she was pushing on me. She said that I was practicing "reverse racism" against white men. When I tried to explain how none of her husband's friends had a spiritual bone in their bodies, while the man I was seeing was deeply connected with Spirit, she shot out, "By refusing to go out with suitable men, you are sabotaging any chance of getting married!"

After going to bed that night, Peg's words were ringing in my ear. There was something to them—not her comment about refusing to go out with "suitable" men, but I did wonder about the sabotaging-marriage part. I had my issues with marriage. I had ended three long-term relationships after my partners' push for marriage intensified. While all three men could not have been more supportive of whatever I wanted to do, I had an unrealistic fear of entrapment. My thoughts shifted to my father and how disappointed he had been that I had not married my first longtime boyfriend, whom he had loved. I thought, "You didn't get married until you were fifty-seven, so why expect anything else from me?" I remembered the last time I was with him, how he had relieved me from any guilt about not being married by telling me how my happiness was his priority, and felt my tears flow. I missed him. I thought, "I know you meant it and I know that you are with me, but would you just give me a little sign?"

There was a door on each side of the bed. One led through the bathroom into the kitchen, and the other one, which I hardly ever used, opened out into the stairway. At that very moment, that door spontaneously opened, and the room was filled with what I can best describe as a warm glow. I lay there basking in it. I know I wasn't dreaming, because I eventually got up to close the door. I climbed back into bed in amazement and gratitude, falling asleep while still feeling my father's presence.

Several years later, I had started a dress-designing business. I needed money but wanted to avoid taking out a bank loan. My father had gotten me into the stock market when I was nineteen, and I had done pretty well following my father's practice of reinvesting the dividends. While walking home from my studio, I was mulling over selling some of my Boeing stock, which was at a high, and felt my anxiety mounting. I wished my father were here to advise me on what to do. I tried to second-guess him. My gut was telling me to sell, but I needed confirmation. As I unlocked the door of my building and started up the stairs, I looked up, asking, "Daddy, won't you give me a sign?" When I reached my fourth-floor apartment, my jaw dropped. The door to my bedroom was wide open. The last time I had seen it open was when it opened by itself after I had asked my father to affirm that he really meant what he had told me the last time I saw him before his death—that my happiness took priority over whether or not I was married. I just stood there in awe, staring at the door, thanking him. There was no question in my mind that my father was giving me the green light to sell!

THE VISIT

The experience I had with my father that felt the most real was when he visited me in a dream. I was panicking about something, most probably about money again. I had inherited my fear issues over money, or the lack thereof, from my father. A bounced check could plummet me into irrational catastrophizing. It was in this state, after I fell asleep one night, that I had a dream that seemed as real as I am sitting here writing:

> *My father could not be jollier. He's hugging me tightly. As he lets go, he points and wags his finger at me, exclaiming, "You wait and see, Dolly. Everything is going to be all right! You just wait and see!" Then he hugs me tightly again. I feel the fabric of his shirt, his cheek next to mine, and his mustache. He lets go and tells me again how wonderful everything's going to turn out. His eyes are twinkling, and he appears giddy with knowing something that I don't. I am thinking, "This is too real to be a dream." He alternates between hugs and bellowing encouragement for at least five full minutes until I wake up overjoyed, without a trace of anxiety.*

Lily Dale

Our friends and neighbors across the street, Mary and Joyce, have a small island off the coast of northern Maine. We timed our visit there with my friend Sandy's daughter's wedding on a gentleman's farm just outside Buffalo, New York. I found out that the state fair and a Beyoncé concert would be held the same weekend, and hotel rooms were scarce. I had a deadline to meet and asked my husband, Frank, if he would book an Airbnb for the night. After some searching, Frank announced that he had found one. "I booked a place in Eden, just ten miles from the farm, for two nights!" he proudly chirped.

"Two nights? Why? What's there to do?" I asked, perplexed.

"It's right on Lake Ontario!"

"We're going to cut our time on the island and spend the day looking at a lake?" I asked, more perplexed.

"Listen, it was cheap, and I thought that we could use the day to lie back. Besides, I thought you would find the hosts interesting."

"What's so interesting about them?"

"The husband has been in radio broadcasting for over forty years and is writing a book about it, and the wife does Reiki. She offered to lead us in a meditation in the morning."

"Hmm, I definitely think we should take her up on the meditation, and maybe this is an opportunity to have a Reiki session." We could turn this into a spa day, I thought.

After arriving at the Airbnb just in time to change our clothes for the wedding, we were greeted by our hosts, Anne and George. Anne confirmed our 9:30 a.m. meditation and told us she would be leaving at 10:30 a.m. to do a book signing in Lily Dale.

"You're doing a book signing? How far away is it?" Anne had my attention.

"About forty minutes. It will be at the bookstore."

"Is Lily Dale a town?"

"No, it's a gated community," she explained, then added, "It's a spiritual community."

"We would love to come to your book signing," I said as I shot a glance at Frank, who nodded. This certainly would beat staring at a lake.

Once we arrived at Lily Dale and entered the gate, we were in Americana perfection. We meandered through the manicured grounds of this parklike community with tiny multicolored cottages, white picket fences, and flowering rosebushes. It felt as if we were on a Victorian stage set. Quite a number of people were walking around with contented smiles. What was this place? At the bookstore we found Anne signing her book on Reiki. She introduced me to the bookstore manager and told her that I was writing a memoir about the miracles I had experienced.

"That's just up our alley," said the store manager, handing me her card. "Let me know when you've finished it, and we'll give you a book signing."

"Thank you!" I said, pleased as punch. This is why Frank inexplicably booked the room for two nights and why we ended up here, I thought, so I can have a book signing! "What goes on here in Lily Dale?"

Handing me a schedule of events, the store manager said that it was a spiritualist community where registered mediums came from all over the country and offered private sessions to people who sought to communicate with departed friends and relatives. It was seasonal, and although there were year-round residents, it was open to visitors only in the summer. The store manager suddenly looked up and said, "It's Sunday today. There are two message ceremonies on Sundays, one at two and one at seven."

"What is a message ceremony?" I asked, intrigued.

"People gather in the assembly hall and receive messages through the mediums. It's free."

This was too good to be true. I turned and faced Frank. I didn't have to say a word. He took the cue. "Okay, let's go!"

The weather was perfect. After a stroll and a delicious lunch on a large Victorian wraparound porch, we headed for the assembly hall. We took our seats toward the back so I could get the whole picture and observe people's reactions. There were more than a hundred people assembled. The emcee began with a short description of the "ceremony" and introduced the first medium. Each medium was allotted ten minutes to do two readings and then introduce the next medium.

First, the medium would call on someone from the audience and ask for their permission "to receive." Next came a description of a person that went something like this: "There is a large jovial man who wears overalls and tinkers with cars. He tells jokes and laughs at them. It's an uncle." The recipient would nod excitedly, and the medium would go on to deliver the message, ending with, "Does this make sense to you?" There were only a few times when the description of the departed was not familiar to the recipient. The medium would then respond with, "Well, the message was probably meant for someone else."

I was completely engrossed in focusing on every expression of those receiving messages. Toward the end of the program, the medium pointed in my direction. "You, with the white hair and glasses." I looked around. At least a third of the audience fit the description. Then louder: "You with the green headband!"

"Me?"

"Yes, you. Will you receive?"

"Like a sponge," I answered eagerly.

"There are two men: one is your father, the other is your grandfather, but it's your father who wants to give you a message. He's short and stocky. No, he's short and solid." The medium paused for confirmation. I was in disbelief. The correction hooked me—my father was five feet one but thought he was six feet five and for most of his life was solid muscle.

"That's him!" I blurted out.

"He wants you to know that he's sorry for having said some inappropriate things, and that he is full of love for you." Astonishment. When my father and I would fight, he wouldn't speak to me for days, and I found out after he died that he would tell his friends how horrible I was. Even though I knew how much he loved me, hearing this had hurt me. It remained under the surface but would come to mind from time to time. My father had just made everything right, and I felt truly whole!

"Your father also has a message for your nephew," she went on. Immediately I thought of my nephew John, with whom I have a special bond. "He doesn't want your nephew to find himself on the other side and be sorry for what he did on Earth." It was then that I realized the message was for my other nephew, Nick, who I knew had been going through a dark period.

"Thank you for all of this" was all I could say.

The minute we were in the car, heading for Maine, I called Nick, but there was no answer. The next day I texted him from the island that something strange had just happened—that a total stranger had given me a message for him from his pappou. I told him that I would not deliver it to him unless I had his permission. I had decided to adopt the approach the mediums used when delivering their messages. His response was immediate: "What time is good for you?"

On the phone that evening, Nick opened up about his struggles. I had no idea how much worse things had gotten. He relayed that his wife had left and taken their three kids to her parents' house in Los Angeles. He was in a paralytic depression, and there were guns around him.

After he gave me permission to deliver the message, I told him what the medium had conveyed to me, stressing the message directed at him. "Pappou doesn't want you to find yourself on the other side and be sorry for what you did on Earth. Does that make sense to you?"

After a long pause, he let out a definitive "Oh yeah . . ."

Now there was not a trace of doubt as to why we had

stayed in this particular Airbnb for two nights and why we found ourselves in Lily Dale. We had been invited there by my father. It was nice to be offered a book signing by the manager, but the real reason we were there was to end up at the message ceremony, where my father could make amends to me and reach out to Nick in his time of need. This deeply resonated with Nick and resulted in his turning his life around. I credit Nick for doing the work, but my father's message got the ball rolling. I knew in the back of my mind that my father had been communicating with me with his signs all along, but the experience at Lily Dale confirmed that he wasn't that far away at all.

Thank you for everything, Daddy!

2

MY MOTHER

THE TV

It turned out that taking care of my bedridden mother in the home I grew up in was to be one of the biggest blessings of my life. The ten months I was there, culminating in her transition, were filled with grace. Mother had been living with my brother and his family, and it was time I stepped up to care for her. Frank and I drove from Philadelphia to Portland, Oregon, in a sturdy old clunker we had bought from his daughter and which I could use for errands after Frank flew back home. I had the house professionally cleaned and turned the sunny family room into her bedroom, placing the hospital bed next to the window facing the dogwood and fruit trees. It was now ready for her to come home.

From the get-go, everything magically fell into place, as if the Universe was conspiring to provide exactly what we needed. The high cost of round-the-clock caregiving had substantially depleted Mother's finances. Extra money came from an agency supporting in-home caregiving. Mother was evaluated and found eligible to receive hospice care. When the hospice nurse and chaplain showed up every week, it was as if angels were visiting. Doris, another earth angel, appeared in our lives. Fully funded by insurance and hospice, she came every Tuesday and took over caregiving for a full twelve hours, giving me much-needed respite.

I had found Mother to be more frail since I had last seen her, but day by day her color improved, and she was getting strong enough to stand while holding on to the bed rail. We soon had a routine. Every morning I gave her a hot-towel facial and a shoulder massage, followed by prayers and breakfast. Her three-hour afternoon naps allowed me to do errands and to write. Three of her close friends came over every Tuesday morning to have coffee with her. Her weekly highlight was every Thursday evening when my nephew John would come over to have dinner with us and put her to bed. If she was having a good day on Sunday, I would dress her in her classically tailored clothes, replete with hat, get her into her wheelchair, and take her to her church several blocks away. When she wasn't up to it, I would have her priest come to the house to give her Holy Communion. Mother was perking up.

Curious things began to happen from the very beginning. A pair of blue jays lived in one of the fruit trees in the backyard. In the mornings when Mother and I would be having breakfast on the front porch, one of them would sit on the railing. No matter how many times I went in and out with the door slamming behind me, the blue jay never moved. As soon as I brought Mother inside, it was gone. Similarly, a cat from across the street seemed intent on stealing into the house every chance she got and managed to make it in twice. Both times, I found her at my mother's bedside.

One of the most inexplicable incidents had to do with the television. I found a heavy old Philips TV at a nearby thrift store. John carried it into the house, and we plugged it in. There was no reception on any of the channels except for some still landscapes. I called Philips headquarters with the model number and was informed that it was a hospital room TV. The part required to convert it into a regular TV cost seventy-five dollars. When I told them that I had paid forty dollars for the TV and that it was for my ill mother, whom I was taking care of, they sent the part for free. I took the TV apart and followed the directions, even calling Philips back for coaching, but nothing worked. I called nearby Providence Hospital and talked to their television technician. He kindly offered to come over after work and install the part. After taking less than five minutes to make the TV work, the man informed me that this model did not receive cable, only broadcast channels. I relied on cable news, but the TV was for Mother, and two of her favorite shows, *Jeopardy!* and *The Rosie Show*, were both on broadcast channels. After the technician left, I turned on the TV and mysteriously had access to all the cable channels! Rosie O'Donnell's show had gone off the air, and Mother showed indifference to *Jeopardy!* I accidentally found out that she was intrigued by hockey and extreme sports competitions—the more action, the better! When I told the hospice staff about the serendipitous occurrences, they told me that these types of things happened to their patients all the time.

THE POTTY

We had our routine down. With time, however, Mother became more and more withdrawn, and eventually her friends stopped coming to visit with her. The more ethereal she became, the more I felt there was an angelic presence. Typically in the morning, after her hot-towel facial and prayers, I would stand her up and pivot her onto the potty next to her bed. She had become constipated, and I had started giving her a laxative tea every other day to regulate her. It never failed. One morning I was surprised to find that the tea had not worked. Mother appeared too weak for me to get her out of bed, and I decided to forgo the potty. When I saw that she was wincing and struggling, I thought that getting her on the potty would help. She could hardly sit up in bed. Determined, I tried standing her up. Just as she was crumpling on me like deadweight, I managed to drag the potty with my ankle and place it under her. As I was trying to keep her on it, she was slipping and her arms were sliding off me. I knew that I could call 911 and ask for "handicap assist" if she slipped onto the floor, but feeling utterly helpless, I raised my arm and shouted out loud, "Help me!"

I will try my best to explain what ensued. I know for certain that I did not pass out, because I was standing, but in the next second I felt that I had come to, as if I had just regained consciousness. The vision before me made me gasp—I literally could not believe my eyes. My mother lay peacefully in bed on her side, facing the window, neatly tucked under the covers. There was no physical way that I could have lifted her onto the bed. There must have been an intervention. Where else could the help have come from than from the angel whose presence I had been sensing? I just stood there in tears, whispering, "Thank you," over and over again.

THE SEND-OFF

For two months Mother had reported seeing angelic children and men wearing flowing robes and sandals in the house. She had lost her appetite, and I had been feeding her, egging her on to have another bite as if she were a child. It felt as if she had packed her bags and had one foot already on the other side. On the evening of September 7, 2003, I made one of my mother's favorites, avgolemono, Greek egg-lemon chicken soup. She hadn't eaten more than a few spoonfuls when she began coughing and couldn't stop. I called hospice, and the woman asked if I would put the phone near my mother. After about thirty seconds, I got back on with the nurse. "Here I am."

"I'm so sorry to tell you this," she said softly. "She's not coughing—it's a death rattle. She's on her way." The acceptance was painful. They would send a nurse at eight in the morning with morphine. I called to tell Frank and then my friend Mary for some spiritual support. I notified my brother and then Doris, her caregiver, who would also be coming in the morning. I really thought that I had prepared myself for this, but that was one of the worst nights of my life; the crushing helplessness was intolerable.

The nurse arrived with the morphine at the same time as Doris, who would be administering it. My brother and sister-in-law came with my niece and two nephews. In the months I had been there, my brother had dealt with our mother approaching the end of her earthly life by ritually coming over to pray with her. Now he was glued to her, holding her hand. When he left to get takeout, I went over to her. Her color was good, and she looked utterly peaceful. Taking her hand, I said, "Mama, I want you to have me in your prayers; you will be in mine forever." A tear rolled down her cheek.

I couldn't even look at the food. About every two hours, I downed a thimbleful of cognac. I let the family be with her while I went out to the patio to call my close friends. George's best friend, Ted, came over to console him. Around seven in the evening, Mother's expression showed some discomfort. When Doris said we should double the morphine dose, I asked, "Is that good for her?" Everyone looked at me as if I had lost my mind. George stayed while his family left for the night. I was emotionally and physically exhausted. I felt immensely indebted to Doris, who said that she would stay until the end. I had not eaten anything all day. George, Ted, and I had a shot of cognac together. Ted left at midnight, and George went to bed in the bedroom next to Mother's. A wave of intense tiredness overcame me. "Doris, I have to get some sleep. I have to."

"Would you like me to wake you when it's time?"

"Yes, thank you," I said as I kissed my mother good night.

Doris came upstairs and woke me up at a quarter to two. I wanted to get up, but I felt delirious. I could hardly put the words together. "I can't move, Doris."

"That's okay. Go back to sleep, I'll take care of everything."

As I lay in bed feeling like I had been hit by a truck, I felt a virtual bop on the back of my head, as if someone was trying to get my attention. I had to say goodbye. I literally crawled out of bed, hardly able to move. I went downstairs to find my mother looking ashen. Her breathing had slowed way down. I took her hand, told her how much her love meant to me and how much I loved her, asked her to watch over me, and kissed her. Turning to Doris, I said, "I just can't stay up. I feel as if I'm going to pass out. I need to sleep."

"I've witnessed how you've cared for her and how devoted you've been to her. Go ahead," Doris said, giving me permission.

As soon as I lay down again, I felt another whop on the back of my head. That one literally brought me to my senses. I thought, "What! Mother is about to go on her second-most-important journey of her life—the first being her birth—and I'm going to sleep through it?" Out of nowhere I was suddenly injected with energy. I jumped out of bed and ran downstairs. "Doris, I'll take over. I need to be with her." I had said everything I wanted to say to her and was holding her hand when I felt the third slap to my head. "Doris, go wake up George!"

George walked into the room mechanically, like Frankenstein's monster. "George, take her other hand!" I directed as if reading a script. What I heard coming out of my mouth was not from me but from another, much greater director. "Mama, I am holding your hand, and George is holding the other, just like we did when we were little. Go! Go forward toward the light, where all the angels are there to welcome you, and Daddy's up in front waiting for you with his hand outstretched!" I looked down, and she had followed my directions. It was 2:12 a.m. She had left us, and I knew that she had been welcomed exactly as I had been directed to describe. George doubled over in grief. I fell to my knees, thanking God with all my heart. But there was someone else to thank as well—my father—the generator of those blows to the back of my head, who kept trying to awaken my awareness so that my mother could have the transition she deserved. She had hung on until my brother and I were with her. How close I had come to missing the gift of a lifetime!

I looked at my mother incredulously for several minutes. She looked remarkably young. All the stress was gone from her face, and her wrinkles had vanished. It was the face I knew as a child. Tears of joy ran down my face, knowing that my mother got exactly the send-off she wanted. She had reunited with my father and was now free to be with the angels and her beloved Virgin Mary.

GARDENIAS

At my mother's funeral, I had pale-colored roses draped around the casket with three gardenias, her favorite flower, nestled in for the powerful scent that she adored.

Eight months after my mother's transition, Frank and I were in Chicago for our friends' son's wedding. Both sets of parents had gone all out. It was one of those big, raucous Jewish weddings with good food and joyous dancing. At one point the tables had emptied, with everyone on the dance floor. Taking a break, I sat at our table alone, watching the festivities. I reminisced about how happy my mother had been at our wedding. Although she wouldn't dance after my father died and would wear only subdued colors, she made an exception for our wedding, wearing a rose-colored dress and dancing with gusto.

I knew where she was—with my father—in perfect peace. As I got up to go to the ladies' room, I asked for a sign of confirmation. Upon entering the stall, I became aware of the fragrance of gardenias. I just assumed that someone who had used the stall before me was wearing gardenia-scented perfume. I went to the sink, and there on the counter was a wide glass bowl with three gardenias floating in water, bringing to mind the three gardenias I had placed on my mother's casket. She was sending me a sign confirming what I had assumed, that she was with my father in perfect peace.

MOTHER MARY

Frank's mother, Mary, was a dear woman with little affect, and another Virgin Mary devotee. I called her *Mother Mary*. She loved talking about the Virgin Mary and Medjugorje, a rural town in Bosnia and Herzegovina, where the Virgin Mary had reportedly begun appearing to six children in 1981, when the town was part of Yugoslavia. Whether or not the apparitions actually happened, they were real to Mother Mary. She even subscribed to a magazine that featured messages and stories about the "seers," now adults. Every time we would visit her in northern New Jersey, she would tell me the latest Medjugorje news. And every time we'd get ready to leave, her parting words were the same, in a monotone voice: "I really enjoyed your company." The last time I saw her, she gave me her rosary from Medjugorje, as if she knew it would be our last visit.

After an extended illness, Mother Mary had come to the end of her life. At her bedside were Frank, her daughter Claire, and her grandson, Jeffrey. Frank was calling me with a play-by-play of the developments until I couldn't stay up any longer. As I lay in bed, thinking of her, I asked my mother to welcome her with an embrace and to give me a sign that Mother Mary was with her. Frank called in the morning to fill me in, and I asked him the time of her transition. He said 2:12 a.m. It was the exact time my mother had made hers! My mother had let me know that Mother Mary had joined the Mothers Club in heaven.

VIRGINIA

After my friend's twenty-six-year-old daughter's cancer had spontaneously disappeared the day after I had asked my mother for her intercession, Father Stephen began praying to my mother, referring to her as Saint Anna.

In all Eastern Orthodox churches, between the sanctuary where the altar is located and the congregation is the iconostasis, a screen of prescribed icons of saints and religious paintings in the same placement in all Orthodox churches. In the center are the royal doors, where the priests emerge and retreat during the liturgy. A large icon of the Virgin Mary is always placed just to the left of the royal doors. From the vantage point where I regularly sit, the Virgin Mary in the icon at Father Stephen's church looks just like my mother. In honor of her and the Virgin Mary, before filing out, I step up to venerate it at the end of every service.

I had made plans to fly to Portland, Oregon, on the Wednesday before Palm Sunday for one of my regular visits. It was the Sunday before my trip, and I still had not yet scheduled dates with family and friends. Frank and I had gone to church, and at the end of the service, I went up to venerate the icon of the Virgin Mary. As I stepped down to join Frank in line and file out, Father Stephen beckoned to me. I went up to him, and he placed a small, rather unusual brass cross dripping in oil in the palm of my hand, saying, "This is Efkeleo [Holy Unction]; somebody needs it." A bit perplexed, I thanked him, and without another word he smiled and turned around to go back into the sanctuary behind the iconostasis.

It is believed in the Orthodox Church that Holy Unction has healing properties. The priest anoints the congregants with it during the Wednesday-night services before Easter. Years before, I had experienced a healing after dabbing some on a hard lump on my eyelid. The lump had been there for eight months, and it spontaneously vanished.

I told Frank what had just happened with Father Stephen while anointing both of us with the oil from the cross. I wrapped the cross in a paper napkin and put it in my bag, wondering out loud, "Who could this be for?" Neither of us knew anyone who was sick enough to require a cross slathered with Holy Unction.

The next day I was on the phone, scheduling dates with friends in Portland, and was calling Virginia, who was very fond of my mother. She and her husband, Franklin, a retired ex-professor of mine, were old family friends, and we had a tradition of meeting for Sunday brunch. Virginia answered the phone, exclaiming, "I can't believe it. I was just about to call you!"

"About what?" Virginia never called without good reason.

"I'm going in for surgery on Friday, and I wanted you to know."

"What kind of surgery?"

"Heart. It's my heart."

"Oh, Virginia, nowadays the medical field has these procedures down pat—it's pretty much in and out."

"I don't think so," she said, taking a deep breath. "They're breaking my sternum for this one."

The conversation took a somber twist. "What? How long will you be in the hospital?"

"The doctor said at least five days."

"Well, then, I'll come to see you!"

"You're coming all the way from Philadelphia to see me?"

"No, I called to tell you that I'm coming to Portland and to see if we can have brunch on Palm Sunday. Since you'll be in the hospital, I'll come to see you there."

"Oh great! But what bad timing with Easter and all . . ."

Easter! That's when I made the connection with the cross and the Holy Unction. "I have something for you, Virginia." I told her how Father Stephen had given it to me. She asked if she could have it before the surgery, which was scheduled for 6:00 a.m. that Friday. The only window of time that she and Franklin could meet with me was between 2:00 p.m. and 2:20 p.m. Thursday afternoon. I had planned to take a walk and have coffee with Betty, my childhood friend, but since Betty had also known Virginia and Franklin for years,

I proposed that the four of us meet for coffee.

Betty offered to pick me up. "What made him give it to you?" Betty asked quizzically after I told her the story in the car.

"I don't know. I never asked him. If Father Stephen asks me to jump, I jump."

"You didn't ask him? Well, I want to know why, so call and ask him now!"

Father Stephen had indeed singled me out to give me the cross. Why hadn't I asked for an explanation for something so unusual? I called him from the car. I told him about Virginia's and Betty's inquisitiveness. Now I was curious as well.

He said that one of his parishioners had visited their native country, Georgia, and had brought him back four brass crosses. "Thank you for telling me," he said. "Now I know that all four of them went exactly to whom they were supposed to go." And in a completely matter-of-fact tone, he continued, "As far as why I gave it to you, I had one cross left. That Sunday I was walking past the altar, where there is a small icon of the Virgin Mary, and as I glanced at it, I heard your mother say, 'Give this to Sophia,' so I did."

I was awestruck; he had received the message from my mother in the sanctuary at the exact moment I was venerating the icon on the other side of the iconostasis . . . and he acted on it! In spite of all the communications and miracles I have experienced, what continues to surprise me is my acceptance of Father Stephen's acceptance that this type of thing is normal everyday reality.

Betty and I met Franklin and Virginia at a café, and I gave her the cross. After the surgery, Franklin sent out emails on Virginia's status. Instead of a five-day hospital stay, Virginia was in and out of the ICU for a total of eighteen days. It was touch-and-go, but she ultimately bounced back.

I will never know how much the cross with the Holy Unction had to do with Virginia's surviving the surgery. It could have been the surgeon's skill that saved her life. Does it matter? Being privy to this string of synchronicities filled me with joy and gratitude. It is one thing to have Father Stephen give me the cross because my transitioned mother told him to and then proclaim that someone was in need of it. It is another thing to speak to a dear friend, who loved my mother, the very next day and find out that she needed every possible encouragement before her operation. It is yet something else to have already booked a flight to where Virginia lived, and within twenty-four hours of landing to be able to put the token in her hand before she went in for surgery the next morning. Regardless, the convergence of people, places, and things, at the very least, brought Virginia the comfort, optimism, and spiritual courage she needed to face her fear and uncertainty.

TEDDY

How lucky for me to have found out about this story just before the book is published!

Although my nephew John believes that every miracle I have experienced and written about did happen, he remained a staunchly self-avowed atheist. We had opposite political viewpoints but we could still debate issues even as our voices reached crescendos. However, any attempt at a discussion about God went nowhere. Like a light switch, just the mention of the word would turn him off and his eyes would glaze over. On the rare occasion when we could talk about matters ethereal, I would use the word, consciousness.

During a recent conversation, John and I were going over the string of serendipitous events that had landed Frank and me in Lily Dale where a medium had given me two messages from my father, one for myself and the other for my nephew Nick, John's brother. After he commented on how both messages were uncannily relevant and agreed that it would have been impossible for this communication to have taken place without the existence of consciousness, I posed my question:

"We know that you need scientific proof before believing

anything, yet, you believe that all of my miracle claims, that are considered to be anecdotal and paranormal, have indeed happened. So, I have to ask—is there any room, ANY room in your mind for you to consider that something may exist that is bigger than you?"

After a period of dead silence, he responded, "I haven't told you this before." Well, if anybody wants my 100% undivided attention, this phrase guarantees it. "Actually," he continued, "I haven't told anyone."

"OK, tell me."

"When Ted (John's oldest son) was one and a half, and I know he was one and a half because that's when he started talking, he could only say 'Mama' and 'Papa' When we tried to introduce other words, he would try to formulate them with guttural sounds. One day, it was just the two of us in the kitchen and I was feeding Teddy in his high chair. He would get distracted and I was doing the airplane thing to get him to eat. All of a sudden, his mouth dropped, his eyes widened while fixing his gaze over my left shoulder, and he began giggling. Then, while continuing to stare and giggle he began pointing. I asked him, 'Teddy, what are you seeing?' Without hesitating a second, he said 'Yiayiá!' What was amazing to me was that he didn't have any difficulty saying it—he said it with total confidence like she would have said it."

Yiayiá means grandmother in Greek. Most Greek-American kids call their Greek grandmothers Yiáyia with the accent on the first syllable, but Teddy had said it the correct way with the emphasis on the second syllable. Without a doubt my mother, who had made her transition twelve years prior, had appeared to Teddy and had introduced herself to him. I had another burning question.

"John, look, I wrote a book on exactly this subject. What was it that made you keep this story from me for eight years?"

"I had forgotten about it." he replied. "I was younger then and I was hard-headed . . . but now I'm softer."

Softer?

"John, you know that this wasn't a gift just for Teddy, but for you too. Yiayiá was a real strategist when getting her point across—she would customize her delivery according to whom she was talking. She didn't appear to Teddy when he was with his Russian grandparents or when he was with his mom. Yiayiá chose to appear to him when it was just the two of you. And she didn't appear to you, the non-believer. She appeared to Teddy and he let you know it, and it's taken you eight years to process it . . . "

There was no way that John would have been able to handle my mother appearing to him. Instead, by interacting with Teddy and allowing John to experience something other-worldly and outside his comfort zone, she had sowed a seed. Upon reflecting on it eight years later, John was able to tell me that he had had a change of perception, that his mind had been opened, be it a crack, and began to accept the possibility of the unknown and unseen. My mother knew exactly what she was doing!

Thank you for everything, Mama!

3

BUCKY

The deaths of Buckminster Fuller and his wife, Anne Hewlett Fuller, constitute the greatest romantic love/life/death story I have ever been privy to. They were both twenty-one when they wed, and their marriage spanned sixty-six years. A modern-day Leonardo da Vinci, Bucky was one of the most creative people to inhabit the planet, which he coined "Spaceship Earth." He likened it to a mechanical device that we humans were responsible for maintaining, like an automobile, and committed himself to working for humanity. An environmentalist of the nth degree, he famously said, "We don't have an energy crisis; we just have a crisis of ignorance." Bucky studied nature's patternmaking, which contributed to his invention of the geodesic dome. When he was thirty-two, he spent a year in silence in order to learn to think for himself. He used words like "livingry" and "to-ing and fro-ing," which made him a colorful speaker. Although Anne was astutely independent and "did her own thing," she was his most ardent fan and supporter. They glowed in each other's presence. Their love never wavered. It was the kind of bond that continues for all eternity.

A series of coincidences resulted in my meeting Anne and Bucky at the University of Oregon in 1973. We instantly bonded. After a six-year correspondence, right out of architecture school, I moved to Philadelphia to work with Bucky. He regarded all of us in the office as part of his family. He considered himself a "global citizen" and eschewed retirement, constantly traveling around the world giving hours-long lectures, leaving audiences agog. Returning from some place particularly exotic, he would bring us gifts. Author of twenty-five books, the man seemingly never slept, never tired. Anne hated cooking, and occasionally, when Bucky was away, I would visit her and make a big pot of her favorite food that would last her for days.

Bucky had a deep faith in the intelligence of the Universe, and it was from him that I learned to interchange "God" with "Universe" and "Divine Consciousness," believing that they are one and the same. We both shared the conviction that we don't die, that only the physical body is shed, and that our consciousness lives on.

During my tenure at the office, Anne and Bucky moved to Pacific Palisades, California, to be near their daughter, Allegra, and their grandchildren. When not "to-ing and fro-ing" the globe, Bucky divided his time among his new home in California, the office in Philadelphia, and their house on Bear Island, Maine, where he and Anne summered and went sailing on his boat, Intuition.

My friendship with Anne and Bucky continued via correspondence after I had returned to Oregon in 1981. Buckminster Fuller had been my hero long before meeting him, and now Anne had become one as well. In one letter, Anne gushed that she had just received a dozen long-stemmed peach roses, her favorite, from her "Dear Bucky" on her birthday, a tradition he had upheld since their courtship.

I marveled at the dynamic bond between Anne and Bucky. During the time I was working at the office, I would occasionally take my lunch into the library and go through sections of the "chronofile." It consisted of shelf upon shelf of files containing every piece of correspondence Bucky had received and copies of those that had been sent out. Every so often, I would find tender notes he had sent Anne, prefacing her name with "Darling" and "Lady." It seemed that this great man, who traveled and lectured tirelessly, who kept inventing new ways to save humanity from hunger and lack of shelter, drew his strength from his beloved Anne.

In 1983 I was visiting my friend Sandi in Los Angeles. I had not known that Anne was a cancer survivor. I found out that the cancer had reoccurred and that she was recovering from surgery at Good Samaritan Hospital in LA. Bucky had flown back to be with her. He and I made plans to have tea in her hospital room along with their daughter, Allegra. It was wonderful to be with them again. Anne was in high spirits. I was amazed at how anyone, let alone an eighty-seven-year-old woman, could crack witty jokes about Ronald Reagan so soon after surgery. Bucky was grinning in utter delight. After a lovely visit and saying our adieus, Bucky walked me out of the room and hugged me. As I let go, I saw that he was crying. I felt a lump in my throat. We had said goodbye many times before, but I had never seen him shed a tear.

My ex-comrades at the office kept me informed of Anne's health. She had gotten well enough to go home. Allegra spent many nights with her, and Bucky resumed his travels.

Two months after the surgery, Anne had stopped eating. She was taken back to the hospital, where her esophagus was found to be blocked. The doctors concluded that nothing more could be done for her. Shortly thereafter Anne slipped into a coma. Bucky, Allegra, and her son, Jaime, were at her bedside. Jaime took his grandfather home to get some sleep. During the night, the nurse noted that Anne's vital signs had declined, and Allegra summoned her father back to the hospital. Bucky knew this wasn't going to be a visit, but a vigil.

According to the nurse, Allegra and Bucky were sitting on either side of Anne's bed. Bucky was holding her hand with his head bowed. Suddenly he looked at Allegra and said excitedly, "She's squeezing my hand! She's squeezing my hand! I know it!" As he stood up, he complained of dizziness. The nurse put him on the bed next to Anne's and went out to recruit a doctor. Bucky died on that bed. They said it was a heart attack, but I know it was a broken heart. Anne died thirty-six hours later.

For Anne and Bucky, there was no separation in life and no parting in death. Both of them were spared experiencing the death of the other. I am certain that Bucky had willed his. They were buried together in a family plot in Boston, four days before Bucky's eighty-eighth birthday and their sixty-sixth wedding anniversary. The graves were decorated with greenery brought in from their summer home in Maine and long-stemmed peach roses. It doesn't get more romantic than that.

4

JARED

From the time Jared blew into town in 1983, my orbit in Portland became sparklier. A twenty-nine-year-old architect and powerhouse of energy, he had been an associate partner of the renowned architectural firm of Skidmore, Owings, and Merrill in San Francisco. Well into a recession, close to half the architecture firms in Portland had shut down, and he had been transferred to Portland's SOM office to streamline its operations. The architecture office where I worked was one of the victims of the economic downturn, and I felt lucky to have landed a job as a waitress to ride it out.

Jared's design talent was quickly recognized, and he was hailed as one of the most prominent young architects in Portland. Many of my friends worked at SOM, and I began to hear buzz about his ingenuity and fun-loving nature. When Jared and I met at a friend's party, there was a palpable attraction. It wasn't sexual per se, but a genuine heart-to-heart connection.

At first it was our passion for buildings and design that was the glue, but soon we discovered that we had many other interests in common—history, culture, existential issues, and endless gossip. But more than anything, Jared's creativity made every activity a lot more fun. He bought a spacious, open-plan, Pacific Northwest–style house in Portland's southwest hills and began throwing parties that we would plan and host together. I loved dancing with him, as he would perform his moves with unbridled exuberance. We went to the annual architects' Beaux Arts Ball, he as Buddy Holly and me in a sixties hot-pink, short, chiffon bridesmaid's dress and blond bubble wig. What most attracted me to Jared was his ability always to be in the present moment. Whenever the two of us were together, I had his full attention. Even though the attraction between us was undeniable, he had not made any romantic advances.

Jared invited me as his date to SOM's Christmas party, held on December 12. I decided to take matters into my own hands. I made a black velvet dress. It was extremely fitted, below the knee, with three-quarter-length sleeves and a plunging scoop neckline. The finishing touch was a wide, pink, silk taffeta sash tied into a big bow that made me feel like a wrapped present. My friend Skip came over, and I modeled it for him. He said, "If he doesn't rip that dress off of you the minute he takes you home, he's gay."

Jared brought me home, and upon entering my apartment, we fell into a spontaneous, magnetic embrace. Just as suddenly, Jared said, "I have to go," pulled away, and ran out into the cold dark night. I was bewildered and demoralized. I took off the dress and put my head under cold water. I couldn't fathom an explanation, but I was not going to let this put a dent in our relationship.

That July I went all out on Jared's birthday dinner. For starters, I molded a salmon mousse in the shape of a Byzantine church and trimmed it with slices of green olives with pimentos. The entrée was a whole sea bass en croûte in a braided mille-feuille I had made from scratch and festooned with thin cucumber half-rounds for gills. The flourless chocolate birthday cake with a raspberry sauce was a Julia Child recipe that took the entire morning to make. Throughout dinner I felt something was amiss—Jared, who normally had a voracious appetite, did not eat much. My heart bled, but worse, I would catch him staring off into space. Jared was not "present."

The recession continued to be bleak, and SOM had a bare-bones staff, but I had heard reports that things were a bit better on the East Coast. I didn't want to be away from the profession for too long and decided to move back to Philadelphia and look for work in architecture. Jared's expression was glum when I told him, but he encouraged me in my decision, saying, "I'm the last person that would want to keep you here waiting on tables and squandering your talent."

I arrived in Philadelphia at the beginning of September and moved in with my good friend Alice, who had lived for years with Michelle, the owner of a large Victorian house. The three of us shared a wonderful camaraderie. Jared came to visit in mid-September. He looked sallow and void of his vibrancy. Concerned, I discussed the changes I had observed in him with my roommates. While taking a long walk from West Philly through Center City, continuing south to the Italian market, Jared would tire and have to sit and rest. He would not acknowledge that anything was wrong, but as soon as we returned home, he promptly went to bed to take a nap. Michelle took me aside and told me that she had nosed around in his toiletry bag and written down the names of the many medications he was taking. She had conferred with a physician friend, who told her that they were drugs prescribed to patients with HIV. I could not digest what I had just learned.

During a telephone conversation with my friend Jennifer, one of Jared's coworkers, she confirmed the news. She had just found out that Jared had been diagnosed with HIV the previous December 9, a few days before SOM's Christmas party. That explained Jared's abrupt departure following our embrace, but it did nothing to soften the devastating blow. Back then, it was a death sentence. He quickly became bedbound, and his parents came to Portland to take care of him. A barrage of friends would visit to raise his spirits. I had instructed my friend Jan to tie a long ribbon on a helium balloon printed with the words "I love you," place it in a big box, and bring it to him. Jan reported that after Jared opened the box and the balloon lifted to the ceiling, he expressed disappointment that the balloon had slipped away. After being handed the long ribbon, however, he pulled it down, and reading the sentiment, he delightedly exclaimed, "Leave it to Sophia!"

It was October and I had withdrawn socially. I was grieving the loss of my father, who had died that past June, and now another bright light was being extinguished. My birthday is also in October, and I always go into self-reflection around that time. I wanted to spend my birthday weekend somewhere alone. I could not have been more grateful for my friend Amy and her generosity in offering me her parents' Manhattan apartment overlooking Central Park for the weekend, while they were at their second home in Maine.

The apartment on the Upper East Side was perfect. It had not been updated since the 1960s. There were maps of Maine on the walls, and the worn slipcovers could not have provided me with more comfort. The last time I spoke with Jared was on the day of my birthday, October 14. His father held the phone up to Jared's ear, and in a faint whisper, Jared asked when I was coming to visit him. I lied and said that I would come after my project's deadline at the end of the month. I was hoping that he couldn't tell I was crying as we said our goodbyes. His father got back on the phone. "Hold on. Jared wants the phone."

I heard a barely audible "I love you, Sophia."

"I love you more, Jared." I hung up, thinking, "God, please don't let him die on my birthday." He died four days later without ever telling me that he had contracted AIDS. The memorial was held at Jared's house, where so many good times were had. Since I couldn't be there, I taped my eulogy. It was played at the very end, when I assured everyone there who loved him that it was now party time in heaven.

Years later, while doing my morning yoga accompanied by music on commercial-free WXPN radio, Jared came to mind. Missing him, I recalled that wonderful year and a half we had together—it was as if an awesome force of nature had descended upon our town, and then poof, it was gone. Gone where? Where was that energy? I thought, "Where are you, Jared?"

Just then the radio went dead. I thought that the station must be conducting a test, and the music would resume within a few seconds. It didn't. Could my receiver have died? Annoyed, I stopped my yoga pose and changed the channel. There was no problem with the sound. I changed it back to WXPN. Nothing. Abruptly, a song came on, sung by a woman in an angelic voice. Normally I would tune out a song's lyrics during yoga practice, but now the radio had my full attention. The song, written and sung by Tara MacLean and entitled "Higher," stunned me:

If I could spend my life in awe
Of everything I ever saw
You'd be the one to lift me up
Higher than I am
If the sky came crashing down
You'd be the only star I found
Of all those scattered on the ground
I'd hold you in my hand

Higher
Higher
Higher than I am
So this is where I want to be
From now until eternity
A shepherd of the soul to me
And I will be the lamb
Higher
Higher
Higher than I am
I see you sleeping now
Invincible and golden
There's nowhere else to go from here
Higher
Higher
Higher than I am

Jared had wasted no time in answering my question regarding his existence. The unusually long pause on the radio had caused me to pay attention to lyrics I would usually ignore. Through them, Jared had let me know of his bliss—"So this is where I want to be from now until eternity"—and that he was watching over me.

Evidently, neither Jared's love nor his ability to communicate with me had ended with his physical death.

5

GHEAN

Living a Fearless Life was a twelve-workshop program I had created to enhance self-esteem in at-risk women. The designated speaker for the tenth session, "Facing and Overcoming Obstacles," was Kim Ung. Of all the guest speakers, none could hold the women in rapt attention more than Kim and her story.

Kim was a survivor of the 1975–79 Cambodian genocide carried out by the Khmer Rouge and its brutal leader, Pol Pot. Her childhood was spent amid a civil war between the right-leaning military and the armed wing of the communist insurgent Khmer Rouge. Most of the fighting took place in the jungle and in poor villages, where it was easier for the Khmer Rouge to recruit downtrodden peasants. Others in small towns were forced to join their army. Rural Cambodians began fleeing to bigger cities.

It was not until the Khmer Rouge invaded and took over Phnom Penh in 1975, when Pol Pot seized power, that this lush, paradisal country turned into an unfathomable hell. Pol Pot was set on transforming Cambodia into an agrarian socialist utopia, banning personal freedom and the use of money, on his path to communism. During his four-year regime, Pol Pot carried out systematic genocide, with two million people perishing from starvation, torture, and being worked to death.

One of twelve siblings, Kim was then sixteen years old. The older ones had moved out, married, and had families of their own. Still at home with their parents was Kim; her brother Lee, who was a year older; and her two-year-old sister, Ghean. Immediately after the takeover, Kim's family was given three days to evacuate. They packed up their truck and left Ghean with a relative who would take care of her in a large city nearby. At a checkpoint, they were stopped by soldiers who demanded to "borrow" their truck. Carrying whatever belongings they could on their heads, the family was ultimately forced to flee on foot up a forested mountain, finding themselves among nine other families and an outpost of soldiers. Water was located a mile away. They cut down trees, pooled their tools, and built shelters with thatched roofs that proved to be inadequate protection against tropical monsoons. The families planted a vegetable garden to supplement the rice provided by the soldiers. When the vegetables were ready for harvest, the soldiers confiscated them and ordered everyone to leave. Once again, Kim's family took their basic possessions and headed into uncertainty until they found a remote, self-sufficient village.

Two months later, everyone in the village was notified that they were to attend a mandatory meeting. The local Khmer Rouge leader announced that from that point on, all the children belonged to the governing body. They took the teenagers, including Kim and her brother, to work or to be trained as soldiers. Joining about a dozen other barefoot children from the village, they were led on an excruciating two-day trek to a labor camp. Kim's sandals had ripped. She wasn't used to walking barefoot like the local children, and her feet became blistered and bloodied. The children were given only a scant amount of rice and thirty minutes for lunch, which included cooking time. Using the pot she was carrying, Kim cooked the rice but was ordered to leave before it was done. That night she, her brother, and their young companions slept on the ground without cover in a torrential rain, but they were too exhausted to care.

As they resumed their march to the labor camp the next morning, Kim could see from afar that hundreds of children were building a road. As soon as Kim and her companions reached the camp, without rest or food, they were each given a backpack and shovel and were ordered to join the others and go to work. Kim showed the supervisor her bloodied and blistered feet, pleading to stay behind. A wave of pity crossed the supervisor's face, and she relented—Kim could stay but had to cook for a crew of twenty. This was her break. When it became apparent that she knew how to cook well, she was permanently assigned the job. Meals consisted only of rice with an occasional bit of fish. Kim soon discovered that the supervisor couldn't read or write, so Kim began teaching her. Slowly a bond grew between them. Six months later, the supervisor was replaced, and Kim was forced to perform hard labor with the others. Food was reduced to nothing; Kim and her comrades had to fend for themselves, scavenging whatever berries or insects they could find. This was how the Khmer Rouge recruited workers to join their army—if they signed up, they would be fed. Kim and four others formed a group that vowed to resist.

Everyone was closely watched. If anyone exhibited prolonged fatigue or illness, they would be called in to the supervisor, never to be seen again. Before they were shot, they first had to dig their own grave. This also served as a warning against any thoughts of escape. One time two boys tried to escape but were caught. A mandatory meeting was announced, and both were shot in front of everyone. They were buried with their fingers sticking out of the earth as a grim reminder of the consequences of escape attempts.

Seeing her parents again was always on Kim's mind. She woke up one morning with an overwhelming urge to see her family. She pushed the thought aside. The village where she had left her parents was more than ten miles from the camp. It had been a year since she had seen them, and she didn't know that her little sister Ghean had been reunited with them. The more she tried to talk herself out of the idea of going to see them, the more the urgency grew. Finally, from the depths of her being, Kim was overpowered by a resounding push to "go!" that she could no longer deny. She decided to wait until nighttime. There was a river that she would have to swim across, and she felt that she needed a companion. Kim managed to convince another girl, who was from the same village, to come with her. At an appointed time, the two girls met and headed off into the pitch-black night.

Arriving at her parents' house, Kim was not prepared for what she found. Her mother broke into tears and collapsed with relief when she saw Kim. Her head was shaved, and she had vowed to keep it shaved until she knew that Kim was alive. Not knowing had taken its toll, and Kim was shocked to find her so thin. Wiping away her tears, Kim's mother then told her that her three-year-old little sister, Ghean, was dying from a severe infection of the colon. She hadn't eaten, moved, or spoken in days. Her mother whispered, "You came just in time."

They entered the room where Ghean was lying on a blanket on the floor. She had been reduced to skin and bones. As soon as the little girl saw Kim, her eyes widened, and the sisters' eyes locked. There was a special love between them. Kim had taken care of Ghean as a baby, and they had slept together before their separation. She scooped up her sister and held her. Kim let out a long, anguished wail as Ghean died in her arms. One of Kim's brothers wrapped Ghean in a blanket and took her up to higher ground to bury her. After hugging her grieving mother goodbye, Kim and her companion set out to walk hurriedly back to reach the camp before dawn.

The Vietnamese army defeated the Khmer Rouge in 1979. Cambodia was liberated, and Kim and her family were able to return to their home. Robbed of her teenage years, Kim was now twenty years old. She had survived one of the cruelest regimes in modern history with stoic courage. Above all, Kim is forever grateful for that inexplicable urge that made her go home in time to hold Ghean before she died. Was Ghean's dying wish to see her big sister somehow communicated to Kim? Because Kim had followed her inner voice, despite the risk of certain death if caught, both sisters received a supreme gift this side of the grave. That's what love can do.

6

HEATHER

I first met Michelle's glorious daughter, Heather, in 1984 when I moved into Michelle's four-story house in West Philly. Cosmopolitan, with rich life experiences that elude most nineteen-year-olds, Heather was temporarily staying with her mother while charting her next big adventure.

My good friend Alice had been one of Michelle's housemates for years. Alice would often have me over to the house for dinner, and Michelle would join us on occasion.

An artist with a penchant for blue glass and exotic plants, with a trained eye for color and sensuously shaped objects, Michelle had turned the house into an eclectic Victorian theme park and the garden into an Eden of lushness. She was a mesmerizing storyteller. Tall, lanky, with long dark hair and exotic features, she was a blatant seductress. She lived through her impulses and was known for her lavish parties. In her midthirties, Michelle had been an acid-dropping hippie and a veteran of two wildly open marriages, each of which produced a child. There was also an endless list of lovers.

Heather was the complete opposite. The offspring of Michelle's first marriage to Menssen, an engineer whose projects took him and his family around the globe, she had inherited her father's Aryan blond, blue-eyed looks. She was pragmatic and cerebral, yet she possessed the wisdom of an old soul. Heather had been born in Peru. When she was two, Menssen was transferred to Jamaica, where the family relocated. Shortly thereafter, he began having an affair with the wife of his colleague, Roger, who worked in the same engineering firm. Michelle and Roger then began having their own affair. The couples swapped partners. It didn't work out for Menssen, but Michelle and Roger ended up getting married and eventually moving to Trinidad.

The island lifestyle more than agreed with Michelle.

Growing up on a California beach, she had always been a water nymph. She soon had a tight group of American friends and divided her time among being in the water, painting outdoors, and dropping acid with her hippie friends. Heather was being raised by an affable, motherly, Trinidadian nanny. Heather was three when her brother Justin was born, and she took him under her wing.

With their children's education in mind, Michelle and Roger decided to move to the East Coast of the United States. Sitting down with a map, they settled on Philadelphia. Arriving there in 1973, they stayed in a Holiday Inn while looking to buy a house. Not knowing the city, Michelle hopped on the first trolley that came along and arbitrarily got off at one of the stops. She was walking through Clark Park in West Philly, where hippies were playing chess, jamming on their guitars, and playing Frisbee with their dogs. Feeling right at home, Michelle struck up a conversation with a man with whom she had made eye contact. Would he know of any houses for sale in the neighborhood? As a matter of fact, he did. The old lady who lived in the Victorian twin adjoining his unit was preparing to put it up for sale along with the original furniture. He offered to show Michelle his twin, which was its mirror image. When she saw it, she could not believe her luck. The lady next door was home and welcomed them in.

Michelle was beside herself. All the original paneling, trim, tiles, marble sinks, and leaded-glass windows on all four floors were perfectly preserved. She ecstatically made the lady an offer and procured an agreement of sale on the spot.

It didn't take long for Michelle to accumulate a kaleidoscope of artists, New Agers, and affluent flower children in her circle of friends. Good old Roger ran off with one of them and moved to the suburbs. Heather and Justin attended a Catholic school in the neighborhood. Michelle had discovered a newfound independence from men. It was the first time in her adult life that she was not shadowed by a husband. She plunged into self-actualizing by doing whatever she wanted, whenever she wanted, losing any trace of the need for approval. Meanwhile, men were lining up at the door. There was even a brief fling with Abbie Hoffman, who with Jack Kerouac, Allen Ginsberg, Ram Dass, and others heralded in the Beat Generation. In time, the roles had reversed, and it was Heather who had taken on the parenting role, doling out sage advice.

Heather was showing a great interest in horses. Every weekend she would ride the bus to the Main Line on her own to take horseback-riding lessons. She was soon emerging as a skilled equestrian, particularly in dressage. Menssen offered to give her private riding lessons, her own horse, and an English education in Jamaica. She eagerly agreed. Now instead of summering in Jamaica with her father, she would spend summers in Philly with Michelle.

After Heather had graduated from high school in Jamaica, her father was transferred to Colombia, South America. She had been staying with her mother for several months when I moved in. With her long blond hair and perfect athletic physique, she was a vision to behold. What made the greatest impression on me was her eyes. These two huge blue pools would reach deep into your soul, like those of an ancient yogi. Anything she touched, she mastered. Not yet twenty, she was lunch manager at both locations of one of Philadelphia's restaurant-renaissance eateries. As Heather left home for work on roller skates in the morning, picking up speed, weaving between cars, her golden ponytail flinging wildly from side to side, she brought to mind a Valkyrie, one of those mythological female Viking figures who select who lives and who dies in battle, usually portrayed as lovers of mortal heroes.

The career Heather finally decided to pursue was that of an aesthetician. Menssen sent her to Champneys Beauty College, a renowned beauty-therapy training school in Tring, England, an hour outside London. The college guaranteed its students a job upon graduation, but Heather didn't need to seek a job through the school. Her father helped her set up a spa in Colombia, which became so successful that it employed thirty beauticians.

At age twenty-three, Heather was definitively the total package. Natural blondes with blue eyes were a rarity in Colombia, and she was the honey to a bevy of men who swarmed around her like flies. Her boyfriend, the scion of an immensely wealthy family, flew around in his private plane, overseeing his father's businesses, and taught Heather how to fly it. She hired a manager to run the spa. For the next two years, she and her boyfriend were living the high life, flitting off to idyllic beaches and enjoying the finest food and wine. A fly, however, was about to spoil the ointment. Raging gang wars over cocaine and kidnappings by drug lords, hired hit men, and Marxist guerrillas were surging. Fearing for Heather's safety, Menssen sent her back to Philadelphia.

From the time she was a little girl, Heather could read people's auras and had developed massage techniques to clear out negative energy. She was working at a top spa in Philly, and word got out about her healing touch. As Heather was amassing a sizable clientele, she met a young man who was visiting from Seattle. Sparks flew. He persuaded her to come live with him. There was nothing holding her back that she couldn't do elsewhere. She moved to Seattle with him and landed a job at the Four Seasons Hotel as a concierge.

Within a few months, Michelle started getting calls from Heather, complaining about the dreariness of constant rain. Having lived most of her life on sun-kissed beaches and swimming in tropical waters, she felt the gloomy skies of the Pacific Northwest deeply affecting her psyche. Michelle could hear it in her voice; her daughter's lilting spirit was slowly being sapped. She promised Heather that she would help her get back to the island lifestyle she so loved. That night, Michelle had a vivid dream of Heather reaching up to the light as she tried to free herself from a bright-green snake wrapped around her feet. First thing in the morning, Michelle painted the image she had dreamed of onto a large canvas.

A week later, Michelle was off to Puerto Rico with some friends for a reprieve from the Philadelphia cold, to paint and bask in the sun. They stayed at the Horned Dorset Primavera, a small, secluded luxury resort with lush grounds sprawled over a hilly terrain near the town of Rincon. The aquamarine water and white beaches were sublime for swimming and sunbathing, and the waves were coveted by surfers from around the world. While walking past the concierge in the lobby, Michelle overheard him telling someone that he was leaving for the mainland to pursue a master's degree. She lost no time locating the resort's owner to tell him about Heather's credentials. They were interested, indeed! She brought the hotel's phone to the veranda and called Heather to tell her about the resort and the soon-to-be-available position. "Get out of Seattle—the rain is a metaphor for your tears. Come here as soon as you can with your résumé. Hear the surf?" Michelle said, extending the phone toward the sea.

Michelle set out on the beach the next morning to explore possible living situations. She noticed a group of hippies selling their handmade accessories and art and was drawn to a green-eyed woman with long black curls, a woman who she swore "had a glow around her." Michelle struck up a conversation. The woman's name was Rebecca. A Romanian artist, she was also a midwife and the spiritual go-to person in the community. Rebecca invited Michelle to her place. It was a compound comprising her residence, a tree house (her studio) built up in a mango tree, and a small house that she rented out on stilts in the water. It was available. It was perfect. Michelle told her she would take it. Even if Heather didn't get the job at the resort, this would be the ideal summer getaway for Michelle.

Heather arrived at the San Juan airport a week later. Michelle picked her up. As they drove through the resort grounds, Heather stared out of the window wide eyed. When she got a glimpse of the hotel and the ocean, she let out a gasp and shot out her intention to the Universe: "This is where I'm working." Heather wore a simple black dress and pearls to the interview. Michelle had done a great job promoting her. She met with the owners and manager, who treated her as if she were already an employee. After they scanned her résumé and gave her a tour of the premises, Heather was asked how soon she could start. "Tomorrow?" she replied. She had already broken up with her boyfriend and instructed him to send her packed belongings to her.

As far as Heather was concerned, she had found her paradise. Before Michelle left to return to the mainland, Heather told her mother how vibrant she looked after just a few weeks of island living. She asked her mother to promise that she would get rid of her house in Philadelphia, which Heather felt was draining her energy, and move back to the tropics. Michelle replied wistfully, "Someday . . ."

Heather, a jack-of-all-trades, had already made herself indispensable, volunteering wherever help was needed, whether on the grounds or in the kitchen. A short time after Heather was hired as concierge, Vijay, a man of East Indian descent, was hired as a chef. There was an instant kinship between them. What began as a friendship soon developed into a deep love. Drawing on Vijay's vast experience in the food business and Heather's managerial skills, they began planning the creation of their own resort. Their resort was also going to have a spa that Heather would run.

Living on a tropical island, in love with her "teddy bear," as she referred to Vijay, she was now preparing to have her dream come true, running her own resort. Heather was on top of the world. Every time she spoke with her mother on the phone, she would thank Michelle for finding her "heaven on earth."

Vijay was planning to make things even better by surprising Heather with an engagement ring. He asked if she would meet him for dinner after his shift. He told her that he was creating a new dish that he wanted her to try. Heather wore her favorite dress, a retro number, with sunflowers, that had belonged to Michelle. On her way to the resort, the rain turned torrential, but Heather couldn't have cared less.

My phone rang. It was Michelle. "Heather is dead. She was killed in a car accident . . ."

The monotone voice trailed off as I dropped the phone. "No! No! No!" I screamed between wails. I dreaded picking up the phone again. What was I going to say to my friend? "I'm sorry" seemed so utterly inadequate. The receiver felt like it weighed a ton. I managed to get something out. "What happened, Michelle?"

"I don't know." The voice without affect continued: "She crashed into a tree. I don't know . . . she's a good driver." This was not the Michelle I knew who was talking. She seemed to be in paralytic shock. She went on to tell me that all the planes to Puerto Rico were full for the rest of the week, but because this was deemed an emergency, she was able to get seats for her and Justin the day after tomorrow. After I got off the phone, I sat limply on the sofa and cried. It was hard to digest that the light of this beautiful spirit had suddenly been extinguished. Although my friend and her daughter had uniquely different personalities, each following the beat of her own distinct drum, the bond between them could not have been stronger. The love they shared was unconditional as they helped each other navigate through life. The life of one of them had just been cut short.

After arriving in San Juan, Michelle and Justin went to pick up their car. The agent at the rental car company expressed sympathy and comped the car. They were met by Vijay at the resort. He appeared to be lost. It was he who had called Michelle with the news. He told her of the upended surprise he had planned. Heather's friends who lived across the street from where the accident occurred had rushed out after hearing the crash. They had recognized it was Heather and called the hotel to find Vijay.

Heather's body could not be cremated without being identified by next of kin. Michelle and Justin went to the morgue. It was evident that the skull had been dented and cracked. She was still wearing the dress with the sunflowers.

As grim as it was, seeing her daughter's body helped Michelle accept the reality. Heather's father arrived later in the day. The cremation was held up until he could view his beloved daughter's body.

Everyone in the community gathered together on the beach to celebrate the life of a dazzling young star and give her a good send-off back into the Universe. Friends brought flowers from their gardens. Michelle's green-eyed friend Rebecca, the spiritual guru in whose little house on stilts Heather had been living, officiated at the ritual. Vijay was inconsolable, keeping to himself with a bowed head. Michelle encouraged him to join the family and friends as they tossed flowers along with the ashes into the sea. It was then that Michelle realized that the dream she had had of Heather with a snake wrapped around her feet, reaching up toward the light, the image she had painted upon waking, represented her daughter being released from the coils of mortal life.

On their last evening on the island, Michelle and Justin drove to the spot where the accident had occurred. Amid lit votive candles, a stone cross stood at the side of the road with Heather's photograph. Standing there, they tried to make sense of what could have caused the crash. Returning to the car, Michelle turned the key in the ignition. The car wouldn't start. She tried again and again—nothing, not even a click. “Heather doesn’t want us to go,” Michelle said, resigned. Just then, the car spontaneously began honking, and the speedometer vacillated until it went up to sixty miles per hour, when the honking stopped. They both gasped.

Justin spoke up. “Mom, she was going sixty when she lost control of the car in the rain.” The car began honking again, and once more the speedometer reached sixty and stopped again. Heather was confirming her brother’s guess! They sat there speechless until the friends who lived across the street came over, curious about the noise. Michelle and Justin abandoned their vehicle, and the friends drove them back to the resort.

Michelle and Justin were up most of the night, marveling at the communication from Heather. The horn’s inexplicable honking and the speedometer’s moving to indicate 60 mph—when the car’s electrical system wasn’t working, she had cleverly let them know in no uncertain terms what had happened—that she had been speeding in treacherous conditions. This incredible gift from their beloved Heather freed them from anxious speculation, bringing them real closure.

7

OUT

I had no idea that my friend Mary had become addicted to alcohol and drugs. Best friends since our early twenties, we did more than our share of drinking and partying in college, though we never got really sloshed. What kept me from getting drunk was my dread of throwing up. I was also not a good druggie candidate. Normally extroverted, the few times I smoked marijuana I went inward and became antisocial. Marijuana and I were not a good match. One time I took some speed that a friend had given me to pull an all-nighter studying for finals, then took a little bit more in the morning to wake me up before the exam. As soon as the exams were handed out, I started feeling weird, with symptoms of a severe panic attack. I told the professor that I was feeling sick and fled. Luckily I was able to take the exam at a later date. That was the end of my flirtation with speed.

After moving to Philadelphia, I would visit my friends and family in Portland three times a year. Mary had a son, Brenden, from her first marriage and was a fantastic single mom. On each of my visits, however, Mary and I would spend one night staying up all night snorting cocaine, playing backgammon, and laughing hysterically. We would go to bed for a couple of hours in the morning. Every time, after waking up, I would feel horrible, wanting to crawl out of my skin, vowing never to do that again. I never did cocaine with anyone else, and I believed that Mary didn't, either; I thought it was our little thing. One time we did it the night before I was flying home. I had left renewing my Oregon driver's license to the last minute and made Mary drive me to the DMV. I was wearing a red turtleneck. The background where I had to stand was also red. I looked like a dead person in the photo, with only the whites of my eyes showing, and they would not retake it. For the next ten years I cringed every time I was asked to show my driver's license with that awful photo. I never did cocaine again.

If I had to describe Mary with one word, it would be "effervescent." Beautiful, quick witted, with a lilting laugh, she was always on and great company. We were on opposite coasts but talked on the phone almost every day. I hadn't noticed anything out of the ordinary in Mary's behavior until after her mother's death. She seemed to be pulling away. Her calls became less frequent, or she wouldn't return mine. She always had a good excuse. She moved in with her boyfriend, and the relationship sounded abusive. Now I was starting to get concerned, for both her and her son.

There were two incidents when Mary's behavior struck me as very odd. During what seemed to be a normal conversation, she dropped a bomb—telling me that she had cancer and asking me to lend her $1,000 to help pay for an operation. Although this was someone I trusted with my life, something told me to hold back and give her only an amount of money that would not make me feel resentful if she didn't pay it back. I gave her $500. I didn't hear anything more about cancer after that. When I asked her about the operation, she told me that she had read a book on self-healing and followed the recommendations, and the cancer had gone away. She never paid me back the money. On my next visit, Mary listed all the reasons she couldn't spend time with me but would stop by my mother's house to say hi. She was always well dressed and had a great haircut. This time, her appearance scared me. She was wearing overalls, and her hair, dyed a mahogany color, was in pigtails with a permed fuzzball on top of her forehead. She looked like a human poodle. I asked her what made her do that to her hair, and she replied curtly, "Because I like it."

Why was I reacting with fright at seeing Mary's hair? I couldn't put my finger on it. A memory emerged. In college, my friend Linda had long, thick, lustrous black hair she maintained beautifully. She was diagnosed with bipolar disorder. A month before we both were to graduate from architecture school, she cut it short jaggedly. A few days later she committed suicide. For me, really bad hair is not a good sign.

Mary stopped communicating entirely with me after that. I repeatedly left voice mail messages on Mary's phone, imploring her to call and give me some clue why she had pulled away. I had no choice but to let her go.

On May 12, 1996, Mary left me a voice mail message, asking me to forgive her for her disappearance. It had been three years since I had seen her and we last spoke. I called her back immediately and told her that I would not forgive her, because there was nothing to forgive. She told me that she had gotten sober on Mother's Day the year before and had been in recovery. She had waited to call me on her sobriety birthday. Mary proceeded to relate her harrowing story of addiction and attempts at recovery. She had begun drinking heavily to cope with her mother's death and found herself on a downward spiral of addiction to heroin. I heard about her abusive boyfriend she was no longer with, her denial, and the tight grip the disease had had on her. She said that she would say and do almost anything to get drugs. Now I knew how the $500 I had given her for the "operation" had been used. Fortunately, her son had gone to live with one of Mary's sisters while she was in recovery. I realized how close she had come to dying. But now I was elated—my best friend was back, as wonderful as ever!

The youngest of eight siblings, Mary was the apple of her father's eye growing up in Eugene, Oregon. I loved her parents, William and Mimi. Ever affable and entertaining, Mary's father was known for his droll quips. His wife called him Dut, short for Dutton, their last name. He always called Mary "little girl." I can just hear him calling to her in his gravelly voice, "Hey, little girl, how's my little girl with the smile?" He would tease her, then let out a hearty laugh. The special bond between Mary and her father was there for all to see.

When Dut was dying, he was surrounded by all eight of his children, their spouses, and his grandchildren. At one point, he sat up erect in bed, looked directly at each of his family members one at a time, and then lay back down and closed his eyes. Mary was looking out the window when something told her, "Go sit by your papa." She went over to him and took his hand. Dut opened his eyes, looked at her, and took his last breath. It was October 17, 2001.

By the time of her father's death, Mary had completely turned her life around. She was married to her second husband, and her son, Brenden, was graduating from college. In Alcoholics Anonymous she sponsored several women, was a sought-after speaker, and had become an inspiration to hundreds. Mary was not only my best friend, but she had become my spiritual sister.

Mary was the development director at the Living Enrichment Center, a flourishing spiritual community, and was surrounded by like-minded people. She was in deep grief after her father's death. Mary Morrissey, the center's founder, offered condolences and then said, "Your father will contact you in some capacity in the next few months. He needs some time to settle in on the other side." Mary did not give the comment a second thought.

Two months later, five days before Christmas, Mary was at one of her regular AA meetings. Paul, a member, took her aside and handed her a folded piece of paper, saying, "Mary, these words came to me in my morning meditation. They're from your father." Mary was at a loss. She knew Paul only casually from the meetings. She had shared about her father's death at one of the meetings, but with no personal details.

Mary waited until she got home to open the envelope. In it was a poem entitled "My Youngest Child Mary." Here it is, as it was written:

A season of joy is upon us again
A little "Savior" was born in a faraway land
His life started meekly without much fanfare
A few came to see him from lands far and from near

I am reminded of a child, a little girl from Eugene
Who blessed all of our lives when she arrived on the scene.
The youngest of eight, my little girl with the smile
One that could capture your heart from over a mile

As the years went by and we grew apart in time
I hoped and prayed you'd survive, dear youngest child of mine
The years rolled on, phone calls sometimes came at night
"Hello Daddy," you'd say, "need some money, an operation will make it right"

Your behavior all changed though, one special day in May
I am so grateful now that I continued to pray
I asked GOD to watch over you, to keep you safe and sound
Bring her back, I said, we love her, and want to keep her around

Your life has changed so much since that miracle day in May
I have left for a better place now, that's not really so far away.
So continue on, one day at a time, and don't forget to say
Someday we will be together again there, just remember to hope and pray

I watch you daily now with pride and a puffed out chest
My God you're a lady, and one of the best
I'm always with you my dear youngest Mary
So don't be sad, and for heaven's sake, there's no need to worry

Just remember today as your life continues on
I am in heaven bragging about you from dust until dawn.
To those who will listen about my youngest child Mary,
I say, "Look, that's my girl! There's no more need to worry"

"Let not your hearts be troubled," the Apostle John did say,
"In my house there are many rooms" and a place for me to stay,
So do the next right thing, and please remember to pray
For our separation is only temporary, we'll be together again someday.

During the next few days, Mary reread the poem over and over again, crying. Her papa had come through for his beloved little girl, as Morrissey had predicted. She knew in her heart where her father was and that he was watching over her, but this was the validation she needed to help her with the grieving process. Mary was incredulous. The poem was channeled through a man she barely knew. And Paul had to be open enough not only to receive the poem but also to write it down. She had shared that she had come from a large family, but not the number of siblings or that she was the youngest. She certainly had never shared that she had hit up her father for money for the same "operation" she had asked for money from me. Paul had no way of knowing the personal anecdotes in the poem.

Interestingly, the poem had been lost for ten years, and Mary had never told me about it. Two stories I already had for this book were about the experiences of two other friends. I was secretly wishing for a third. I knew all my friends' stories and had given up hope that a new story would surface.

As I was writing the second friend's story, Mary's son, Brenden, called to ask her for his birth certificate. Opening the file with the birth certificate, she found the poem along with a black-and-white photograph taken at our college graduation. In her cap and gown, the "little girl with the smile" was flanked by a beaming Dut and Mimi. Mary called to tell me about finding the poem. I couldn't believe it—here was my third story to write about from my best friend! I couldn't have asked for anything better or timelier.

Thank you for everything, Mr. Dutton!

8

JOY

Joy, born and raised in the Powelton Village section of West Philadelphia, was a neighborhood character. She was always disheveled. Her thick, longish hair was turning gray. Joy's large, soulful blue eyes disarmed people into showing her respect. Ever since her parents had died, she had lived alone. She would be seen walking her two pugs, one on a leash and the other, arthritic one on a homemade dog cart that squeaked as she pulled it along the pavement. She was basically a bag lady who owned rental properties. One of her vacant properties was three doors down from ours. I would see her hauling boxes and antique furniture out of her beat-up vintage Ford Bronco. Everything about her was vintage. Joy and I met formally at the annual four-block-long Hamilton Street sidewalk sale a year after we moved into the neighborhood. Neighbors would set up tables in front of their homes and, as the joke went, sold stuff they had bought at the previous year's sale. On and around Joy's tables was an eclectic array of items with unusual shapes and designs—leaded-glass windows, furniture, objets d'art, and period jewelry. In her midfifties she may have been unkempt, but she certainly had a keen eye. She was quite personable and told me that she dealt in antiques and vintage items that she bought at auction and sold to dealers. I told her of my interest in antiques, and we began a friendly acquaintanceship. I could not put my finger on it, but there was something about her that seemed off.

Most of the houses in the neighborhood were three-story brick Victorian twins with mansard roofs and gingerbread-trimmed porches. Ornate wrought-iron fences separated the small front yards from the street. Built in the mid-1800s, Joy's twin was colonial in style. Set back with a large front yard, it was a simple brick two-story with a gabled roof and a front porch with white columns. Joy told me that she was adding an extra bathroom in the second-floor apartment that she was planning to rent out to students. She was notoriously cheap, nickel-and-diming contractors, who kept quitting. The project was taking forever.

Joy also had an ornery streak. One day, she had contractors break through the exterior wall of the second story to add a balcony. Not only did it look directly into the neighbor's bedroom, but it was also illegal. Her twin had been designated historic, which allowed for only interior renovations. The neighbors were in an uproar. Ignoring them, Joy continued the balcony construction, installing french doors. She felt that not being able to make changes to the exterior was unfair. Why could the identical twin connected to her house, but not historically designated, be renovated, but not hers? I told her that I saw her point. After the neighbors had an attorney send her a threatening letter, Joy became so infuriated that she stopped construction and ceased to maintain the house. Soon it was surrounded with weeds as tall as trees, which her next-door neighbor would periodically cut down. Creating a dreadful eyesore was Joy's payback.

Joy continued to be friendly with me, stopping while walking her dogs to complain about the neighbors. In time, I began to observe a slow deterioration in her behavior. I knew nothing more about her other than that she lived alone, never cooked, hated vegetables, and lived on "sammiches" from the neighborhood deli across from where she lived.

One day Barbara, a neighbor, sent out a blanket email to members of our community, informing us that Joy was in the hospital a few blocks away. She had been found lying in the street, unconscious. Since Joy had no living relatives or friends, would anyone know how to contact Martha, a lawyer and friend of her mother's who took care of Joy's legal matters?

What jumped out at me was that "Joy had no living relatives or friends." It was a gut reaction—my life was rich with family and friends, and this idiosyncratic woman had no one? I grabbed my coat and went to the hospital. Though she was incoherent, it was apparent that Joy had recognized me and seemed pleased to see me. The doctor would not provide me with information about Joy's medical condition because I was not family. I managed to convince the staff that Joy had no next of kin, that I was a bona fide neighbor and friend, and that someone in the community needed to know what was wrong with her in order to help her. I was then told that Joy had been diagnosed with MS and that she had suffered a severe seizure.

The next time I visited Joy at the hospital was with Barbara. She had the SPCA come and take Joy's dogs away. Someone must have contacted Martha, who was also there. In her late seventies, Martha was not your warm-and-fuzzy type. Joy could now speak, and Martha was giving her logistic advice about her properties. I found Martha to be rather pushy.

On another visit Martha was there with another woman, who introduced herself as Tracy, a neighbor of Joy's who had known Joy for more than twenty-five years. Joy had given both of them permission to receive her medical information. We all exchanged telephone numbers. As I was leaving Joy's hospital room, Martha followed me out. When we came out of the hospital, she asked if I would be interested in buying Joy's vacant property on our street. I told her that I wasn't really in the market for real estate and then asked her, "What gives you the authority to sell Joy's property?"

"I'm her power of attorney [POA]. I've drawn up a trust for her to protect her assets. She will have to sell one of her properties to pay her bills," Martha explained matter-of-factly. "Would you at least like to see it?"

"Sure," I said with an underlying curiosity.

As we walked to Joy's twin, where she had abandoned construction, Martha told me that Joy owned four other properties. Two of them, including the one where Joy lived, had apartments that were rented out to students. There was also the large Victorian home that Joy had grown up in and was now vacant. Joy had begun accumulating her properties by using the family home as collateral. All the buildings were in the neighborhood except for the shore house, which had also remained vacant.

We approached the porch with the white columns, wading through overgrown weeds. As Martha unlocked the front door, she warned me that Joy was a major hoarder. It was shocking. Boxes upon boxes of stuff lined the walls. There was furniture, much of it broken, mixed in with artwork, quilts, rugs, and antique dolls piled in heaps in each of the rooms. There was only a narrow meandering pathway to move through. I noticed that there was no kitchen. It became evident that, aside from punishing the neighbors, Joy had stopped renovations because she had run out of money.

Waiting at the bottom of the steps, Martha said, "You are welcome to make an offer."

"I don't think so. But what if I did buy it? What if Joy comes out of the hospital, finds out I own her property, and gets angry?"

Martha cocked her head and, leaning her face directly in front of mine, said, "Sooooo?" I found her response rather chilling.

A doctor called me from the hospital to tell me that Joy was being released with antiseizure medication and that she would need some monitoring. I called Tracy and Barbara, and we met to strategize on how to help her.

Joy was functioning, but there were some notable changes. She was mixing up her words, trying out different ones until she found the one she liked. I brought her some food. Even though I had been warned, I was appalled at the state of the apartment in which she lived. There were clothes, papers, and stuff covering the floor a foot deep. Moldy food was scattered about, and I detected traces of feces. On the floor was a mattress soaked with urine. The stench was overwhelming. I asked her where she kept the tenants' leases, and, remarkably, they were neatly stacked in a drawer and all perfectly legal. Remaining standing, I was blunt as I gestured, fanning the room with my arm. "Joy, is this really okay with you?"

"Frankly, yes." She didn't mince words either.

About a year after I first went to see Joy in the hospital, she was sitting at my dining room table having vegetables for lunch. Despite her antipathy toward them, we discovered by accident that she liked Indian curry. My interaction with Martha, which I had found disturbing, came to mind. "Joy, do you remember signing any kind of legal document with Martha?"

"Yes, it was something that's supposed to help me."

"Joy, call her up right now and ask her to send it to you." She did. I made her promise to bring me the document when she received it.

Joy brought over the document she had received from Martha. It consisted of two pieces of paper—a generic cover letter and the signatures page. "Joy, there are twelve pages missing. Call Martha up right now and ask her to send the rest of the documents." Again Joy complied.

When Joy came over with the missing pages, I was dumbfounded. Twelve pages had been reduced to the size of postage stamps and printed on one sheet of paper. I immediately called my friend Miriam, a lawyer who worked at an elder-law firm. She asked me to fax it over to her. Twenty minutes later, Miriam called to tell me that she had enlarged the twelve pages and had shown them to her boss. It was the most egregious document either of them had ever seen. Martha surreptitiously had Joy sign over her properties to Martha's son, on the pretext that it was a trust to protect her assets. In reality, Martha had stolen Joy's properties. Miriam's boss sent a letter to Martha notifying her that her POA had been revoked and that the document was null and void. Martha was not foolish enough to contest, and the properties were returned to Joy.

Joy's condition was deteriorating. Although she had assets, Joy was losing control of her empire. The rent money she received was not enough to pay her mounting bills. Some of the tenants were not paying the rent, citing lack of maintenance. Her car was falling apart. So were her body and mind. Joy was having trouble walking and began falling, needing assistance from strangers to get her on her feet again. I would beg her to shower. She started having "accidents," and I eventually convinced her to wear adult diapers. She was also getting into minor car mishaps.

Miriam, a devout Jew, had been seeking ways to be "of service." She asked if she could join forces with me to help Joy. That's how our three-person task force began. Miriam, Tracy, and I teamed up. Miriam would be responsible for Joy's legal matters, Tracy would be the property manager, and I would oversee her day-to-day needs—making sure she took her medication, taking her to doctor appointments, and pushing proper nutrition, hydration, and personal hygiene. Tracy and I were to hold jointly Joy's POA.

The first thing we did as a team was to meet at Joy's apartment and replace her disgusting mattress. Miriam had brought an extra one she had at home. Having worked with the elderly, Miriam took over. She determined that Joy was having difficulty getting out of bed in time to make it to the toilet. We collected enough plastic milk crates to make a base for the new mattress, and that solved that problem.

Joy had lived by her own rules and resisted change and our help. We found out from some old-timers in the neighborhood about her bizarre childhood. Her mother was referred to as "eccentric" and a "nutcase." After Joy's father had died, her mother had pulled Joy out of high school when she was fifteen because she was "lonely." The old-timers recalled seeing both Joy and her mother walking barefoot in the street. Joy's mother bought and sold antiques at auction and taught Joy to discern periods and styles of antique furniture, jewelry, and dolls. After her mother's death, Joy followed in her footsteps, although she mostly bought and rarely sold, waiting for her items to increase in value. Having lived independently from a young age, Joy fiercely clung to her autonomy and viewed us as nosy intruders no matter what we did for her. There were times when she became downright hostile.

It was stipulated in our POA agreement that we were not to receive one penny for our service. We were not in this for the money, but there were times when one of us would get so utterly frustrated with Joy's fighting us tooth and nail that we would question not getting paid. Fortunately, the three of us were never resentful at the same time and were therefore able to prop each other up.

Bills were mounting and taxes were due. I was able to convince Joy of her dire situation and, with my POA authority, sold her shore house. It was in poor condition due to lack of maintenance, and the proceeds were just a tourniquet to stop the bleeding. All but one of her properties had fallen into serious disrepair.

Shortly after offering to help Joy, Miriam called with an urgency in her voice. "Sophia, I just had a meditation with my mother, and you won't believe what she told me. I need to tell you in person. May I come over?"

"Of course!" I was intrigued. Miriam had told me about her mother, Hope, who lived in Montana. A woman of advanced spiritual enlightenment, she channeled several entities and would regularly lead Miriam through guided meditations over the phone.

Sitting on the sofa, Miriam told me that she had not mentioned Joy to her mother. During their meditation that morning, Hope spontaneously began channeling in a different voice. "Joy is not to be perceived by the senses. In a past life, she was in a position of supreme power and abused it. She chose to come back in this life to suffer and atone." This would prove to be a harbinger of what was to come.

Every four months I would take Joy to the neurologist to check for any new MS lesions on the brain. Despite having a string of fender benders, she insisted on driving. The doctor stepped up and reported Joy to the DMV. The next time she was pulled over, her license was confiscated on the spot. Joy's CPA picked her up and drove her home in Joy's car. The steering column and brakes were shot. The car was taken to the dump; one less headache to worry about—Joy killing herself or someone else.

It was February, and my friend and mentor Father Stephen was coming over for one of our bimonthly morning coffees. Father Stephen was instrumental in establishing Covenant House shelters for homeless youth. Much of his time was spent doing outreach in Camden, New Jersey. He had devised a clever strategy of persuading young trafficked women to leave their johns for the shelter. Father Stephen had taken my friend Charlotte and me on one of his missions, and Charlotte had been so moved by the experience that she began volunteering at the shelter. He knew all about Joy. I told him that it was time he saw Joy, my "outreach." Father Stephen and Charlotte were coming over for coffee, and we had planned to visit Joy afterward.

As soon as they arrived, I called Joy to tell her we would be coming to visit. Her speech was slurred. "Something's wrong. We've got to go now." We walked the four short blocks to Joy's apartment. It was eight degrees outside. I unlocked the front door and noticed that the door to her apartment was ajar. We walked in to find Joy on her hands and knees, shivering. There was no heat in the apartment. She was struggling to talk. It was evident that she had had a seizure. Father Stephen covered her with a blanket and ran to the deli across the street to get some hot tea. The stench was too much for Charlotte, who stood in the hallway, watching in horror. While Joy was sipping tea, I called 911.

"No, no!" she screamed, slurring. "I'm not getting into an ambulance!"

I rode with her in the ambulance to the hospital. Late that night, the doctor called to tell me that, indeed, Joy had had a seizure, and that she had almost died that afternoon from a severe urinary infection, hypothermia, and dehydration. The words Hope had channeled during meditation with Miriam hit me—She chose to come back to this life to suffer and atone. What was my role in Joy's story? I wondered. First I saved her property, and now her life?

Joy could no longer live alone. Miriam, Tracy, and I decided that we would sell three out of her four remaining properties "by owner" to save paying the Realtor's fee, and keep the one that was fully rented and needed the fewest repairs. Miriam and Tracy had full-time jobs, and we were all concerned about the time this would take. Miraculously, things seemed to unfold almost by themselves. I called Joy's neighbor, who owned a number of properties in West Philly and whose yard abutted Joy's, to tell him that the building was available. He jumped at the chance. The house down the street from us with the weeds and no kitchen was in terrible shape. A contractor who did a lot of work in the area had once wistfully told me how he would love to live in Powelton Village but didn't think he could afford it. It would be perfect for him since he could renovate the house himself. He, too, was elated at the opportunity. Both buyers paid in cash.

No one was able to get past the vestibule of Joy's large family home, where furniture was piled right up to the doorway. It was packed with years of Joy's hoarding. None of us had time to go through it all. We hired a crew of four to throw out the broken stuff before having an auctioneer come for the rest. There were holes in some of the floors, where you could see the floor beneath. One of the neighborhood old-timers told us that Joy would keep her dogs in the house and not let them out. Mold contributed to the foul odor, and everyone had to wear masks and gloves. We had a Realtor sell the house "as is."

As holders of Joy's POA, we were not allowed to take anything for ourselves unless the item was broken or in the trash. Occasionally I would scrounge through the metal pile to find things to sell at our annual sidewalk sale before the "metal guy" would come by to pick it up. One time I noticed a small box covered with dog poop. Something on it glimmered in the sun. I picked it up with my gloves, brought it home, and hosed it down. It was a golden trinket box with blue enamel on the lid with an N made of what looked like rhinestones. I took it to an auction house to have it appraised. It turned out that the box was French and was made out of real gold! The N stood for Napoleon, and those weren't rhinestones but rose-cut diamonds!

We found a beautifully appointed assisted-living facility for Joy just outside Philadelphia. Amid the treed grounds was what had been a Drexel family mansion. It had a large new addition in a matching architectural style and a carriage house where the vans that provided transportation for the residents were kept. Joy would have her own studio apartment. And now, since she could walk only a short distance with her walker, she would receive physical therapy and round-the-clock care.

After Joy was discharged from the hospital, we took her to her new home. She hated it—hated that she was living with "old people," hated having aides come into her room, and, being a city girl, hated the bucolic setting. She would much rather watch people in the street than look at trees. "I want to go home, I want to go home!" she would scream during every visit. We explained over and over that neither of her apartments in the building she still owned were wheelchair accessible, but that she could go home when she could walk again. With a vengeance she started practicing walking.

For the next three years, I visited Joy almost every week. Frank and I, along with Miriam and her husband, would visit on "family nights." It was evident that she would not be able to walk on her own again, nor was she going to stop missing being in the city. Miriam and I found a facility in Center City, Philadelphia, that had restaurants and a large lobby where Joy could sit in her wheelchair and watch passersby out the window. It was more expensive, but Joy's money was well invested, and, whatever years Joy had left, the priority was an improved quality of life.

Before we had a chance to move Joy, I received a call from her living facility informing me that she had been found unconscious and rushed to the hospital. The doctors said that she might have had a stroke. They would know more after the MRI.

The neurologist called. Joy was unresponsive. A severe seizure that had caused the stroke had left massive lesions on her brain. The medical directive stipulated no feeding tube. He asked that the three of us meet with him. Waiting for us at the hospital were the neurologist, a palliative-care nurse, and an intern. They had the MRI image of Joy's brain on a computer screen. It looked like one giant lesion. When I told the doctor about the facility we had found where Joy could sit in the lobby and watch people out the window, he gave me a pitiful look. "She will never be able to sit up." We were being asked to pull the plug. After being assured that there was no chance of improvement, we agreed, defeated. Joy would cease to be fed. We went to her room and said goodbye. I surmised that God must have deemed that she had suffered enough. Afterward, we went to a bar, where I ordered a double scotch straight up.

The next morning the intern called in amazement. A nurse who was conducting her routine morning check-in reported that Joy had responded to questions with her name and birthday. A second MRI had confirmed the results of the first one, that she was basically a vegetable. "According to the MRI, it is inconceivable that she is talking." Joy would resume being fed. The entire neurology department was befuddled.

Joy was an ongoing enigma. She was eating and beginning to talk. Defying the neurologist's dire prognosis, she was transferred to a facility for physical therapy. I visited her and was surprised at how well she looked. Her speech was stilted, but she was putting whole sentences together. The therapist said that she had actually stood up. More surprising was the change in her demeanor. Her orneriness was gone.

A week later, Tracy and I went to see Joy. We were told that she had taken five steps with her walker. While Tracy was taking a call out in the hall, I went into Joy's room and told her how she had defied the doctors. I told her about the assisted-living facility we had found for her in Center City, and I shared with her that it boasted a variety of restaurants and would enable her to sit in the lobby and watch people. Joy looked directly at me and said, "Thank you. I appreciate you very much!" I was speechless. In the seven years I had interacted with Joy, this was the first time that she had thanked me.

I walked out into the hallway to tell Tracy. Tracy went into Joy's room. She came out as dumbfounded as I was. "You won't believe this," she said, "but after I kissed her goodbye, she looked right into my eyes and said 'I love you.'" Along with her miraculous mental and physical rebound, Joy had become nice.

My routine was visiting Joy once a week, but two days later I happened to be near the rehab facility and stopped by to see her. Joy was ashen. Her breathing was labored, and her eyes were staring out into space. I knew this was it; Joy was checking out. I kissed her on the forehead and said goodbye. I messaged God: "Whatever deal you made with her about coming here to suffer and atone is between you and Joy, God. I'm not going to tell you what to do, but as a human being, I have witnessed her having suffered enough."

The call came at six in the morning. Joy had died during the night. As soon as I hung up the phone, the message I received was crystal clear, as if I had actually heard it—Joy was to suffer and atone until she was able to express love and gratitude. She had just done so with Tracy and me. That had freed her to go to her heavenly home. This explained why Father Stephen, Charlotte, and I had appeared at Joy's apartment just in time to save her life. And it was why she defied the MRI image and the doctors' finding of her being brain-dead. Joy had not yet done what she came back to do.

The Joy conundrum did not end there. We found out that her will had been shredded accidentally. Without another copy, we could not comply with her wishes, and all her assets went to the Commonwealth of Pennsylvania. There was nothing left to attest that Joy Donnelly had walked on this earth. The box with Joy's ashes had sat on Tracy's mantel for weeks, and I could not accept that there was nothing to mark this woman's life. I ordered an engraved brick marker. Frank and I, along with Tracy and her partner, Mills, set out with the ashes and a shovel. There was a small triangular park in our neighborhood with a wrought-iron fence around it, a stone's throw from Joy's house. It was a spot she would look out onto when she sat on her stoop. It honored a local World War I veteran. Joy was somewhat of a veteran too. We buried her ashes and placed the marker. It read "Ode to Joy."

From start to finish, my experience with Joy was confounding. So was the way in which Miriam, Tracy, and I, three people who were not related to her, came together, each tasked to help her in a different way. I recalled what Miriam's mother, Hope, had channeled during their meditation: that Joy had chosen to come back in this life to suffer and atone for abusing power in a past life. It was the only explanation that made sense to me.

I will never have concrete evidence of the forces that brought about these events. What I am certain of is whatever guided me to do what I did was a power bigger than I am. By helping Joy, I had felt the presence of God. Through coincidence, God presents us with opportunities that, when taken, bring what is best for us and for our spiritual growth.

Coincidence also confirms that actions we have taken were on the right path. My adopted daughter, Eleni, came into my life at the age of nineteen, just six months after the first encounter with Joy in the hospital. She, too, had had a twisted childhood, an estranged family, and a biological mother with emotional issues. Most intriguing is that Joy and Eleni shared a birthday, April 3, and were very fond of each other.

Whether these two special women showed up in my life, or I had the privilege of showing up in theirs, I am truly blessed.

9

When It's Not Your Time

I do not consider myself accident prone. Once in a blue moon I'll trip and fall, and every couple of decades I may have a fender bender, but in 2016, within a two-month period, I had two freak accidents that defy explanation. "There but for the grace of God go I" cannot be more aptly applied. It is life changing to believe with certainty that you are about to die. The fact that I am alive today and am sharing these experiences with you has prompted many friends to call both events miracles. What message could the Universe have been trying to tell me?

The first, a car accident, occurred on February 9. I was driving on Lincoln Drive on my way to bring Greek avgolemono soup to my ninety-five-year-old friend and mentor, Rosa Lee. The two-mile stretch of narrow curving lanes, two in each direction, that snake along from Ridge Avenue to West Rittenhouse Street is dubbed "Dead Man's Gulch" for a reason. The number of accidents on that part of Lincoln Drive was legendary, its most famous victim being singer-songwriter Teddy Pendergrass, who lost control of his Rolls-Royce and was left a paraplegic. Until the day of my accident, I had a great time driving on it, pretending I was burning serious rubber on a race-car track even though the speed limit was only 35 mph. The problem was that no one adhered to it.

It was noon and there was heavy traffic. I was driving in the left lane when I saw a huge Lexus SUV barreling around a bend at 65 to 70 mph in the left lane of the oncoming traffic. I later found out that the car in front of it had stopped, signaling a left turn where there was no traffic light. By the time the driver of the SUV realized that the car had stopped and that he was going to rear-end it, he veered across the center double yellow line, coming straight at me. To avoid a certain head-on collision, I reflexively swerved into the right lane and braced myself to be plowed into on the passenger side by a car in that lane, wondering how many cars would be involved in the pileup. The SUV sideswiped the driver's side of my car, sending me spinning in slow motion while I anticipated being hit. The centrifugal force made me feel as if I were on one of those whirling rides at an amusement park, but in slow motion. As I let myself go with it, I sensed something remarkable, a palpable warmth enveloping me like a soft embrace. I thought, "Wow, I'm being protected!"

As soon as the car stopped spinning, facing the opposite direction, any sensation of divine presence went out the window. My door wouldn't open, and panic set in. Fearing the car would burst into flames, I lunged toward the passenger's door. Dazed, I managed to get out. All the cars had stopped, and people were coming up to me, asking if I was okay. I turned toward the SUV. It was about twenty yards away. There were people crouched down, tending to the driver, who was lying on the road. I felt something in my left ear. I touched it and saw a pinprick of blood on my finger, caused by a tiny shard of glass. Incredibly, that was the extent of my physical injuries. I noticed that the airbags had deployed. I walked around to the driver's side to see the damage. The force of the impact had sheared off the exterior sheet metal of the car, and the door was scrunched like a beer can. Sirens were blaring. Fire trucks had closed the road to traffic in both directions. The police and two ambulances had arrived. Two EMTs were trying to convince me to go to the hospital and be checked out. I declined and asked them about the other driver. I was told that he was unconscious and was being taken to the hospital. They looked at the damage on my car, and one of them looked up at me and said, "Somebody's sure looking out for you."

I found out later that the other driver had suffered internal injuries but would survive. Although I had sustained no physical injuries, I was diagnosed with PTSD—I couldn't drive for more than three months and was a terrible passenger, jumping and gasping whenever a car came into my peripheral vision. Apparently divine protection had spread out beyond my car—no other vehicles were involved.

Less than two months later, on March 24, I was taking a walk on the beach in Rockaway Beach, Oregon. My brother and sister-in-law had generously offered me their cozy cabin for a three-week stay to work on my first book. Doubts about my ability to express myself had crept in, negatively affecting the writing. I was stuck. I needed solitude.

The stretch of beach in Rockaway between two inlets is about a twenty-minute walk. It was a bright midmorning as I came onto the beach and turned left to walk toward the southern inlet. A sunny day at the Oregon Coast is always a gift. It was a little chilly, and I was wearing a lightweight parka. A fair number of people were out for a weekday stroll along the water's edge, while dogs happily zigzagged across the sand. I noticed that there was a lot more driftwood than usual. After reaching the inlet, I turned around to walk to the northern one.

The water was ice-cold, and a few brave souls were in it, jumping the waves. Coming upon the inlet to the north, I saw even more debris. An entire tree with its branches smoothed out and polished was lodged on the black rocks between the beach and the road. It looked like an artificial tree sculpture. Several people were standing on the rocks. I was standing on the sand a few feet away from the inlet. Between me and the inlet was lodged a large driftwood tree trunk. The ocean was at least ten yards away. As I watched the waves crash onto the sand, I noticed a wave that looked different. There was nothing wavy about it. It looked like a wall of water similar to a tsunami wave I've seen in photographs, but on a smaller scale. Seconds later, out of the corner of my eye, I saw a ferocious rush of water overtake the inlet, gushing toward me like a flash flood. There was no time to climb the rocks. I wrapped my arms around the dead trunk next to me. The water swirled around me with terrifying power, but I managed to keep my head above it. Hugging on for dear life, literally, I felt the tree trunk begin to lift. “Well, this is it,” I thought. Astoundingly, I faced my certain death with an eerie acceptance. Just then, the water began to ebb, and the tree trunk, my lifesaver, settled back down. The water subsided as quickly as it had emerged. I stood up, covered in sand, tree bark, and seaweed.

The people who had been standing on the rocks ran toward me, yelling to see if I was okay. They seemed shaken as they told me how lucky I had been to survive a “sneaker” wave. As I stood there dazed, they informed me that these waves had been prevalent since severe storms months before had upended the ocean floor, unearthing buried driftwood and scattering debris. About a dozen people had been swept away on the Oregon Coast.

On the way back to the house, I stopped at the grocery store to call Frank and buy rice to try to dry out my dead phone, even though I had no hope, knowing that the salt water had killed it for good. The two cashiers stared at me in shock. I told them about the sneaker wave and asked to use their phone. “Oh, wow,” one said as she handed me the phone. The other one ran to the back and emerged with two yellow plastic placards warning “Caution! Floor slippery when wet,” and placed them on either side of me. I peeled off a wet five-dollar bill from my drenched wallet and paid for the rice. The two women continued to stare at me as I gave Frank, far away in Philadelphia, a cursory report. They watched me leave the store without another word being said.

I began processing what had just occurred, allowing myself to ruminate on how close I had come to disappearing, just like that! Suddenly I became acutely aware that I wasn't cold. To my great surprise I actually felt warm. It was not the same sensation of the divine warmth of protection I had felt during my crash as the car had been spinning on Lincoln Drive a month earlier, but it was definitely odd not to be shivering on a chilly day after being soaked through by frigid water. Yes, without a doubt, just as the EMTs at the accident scene had told me, "Somebody's sure looking out for you."

As soon as I got back to the cabin, I stripped off my clothes and threw them into the washing machine. My entire body was black and blue. The adrenaline had prevented me from feeling the logs and debris that were knocking against me. If I'd had any denial or doubt about the miracle of a tree trunk's saving me from being lost at sea, the bruises were hard evidence.

The next morning I took the bus to the mall to buy a burner phone. When I got back, I called Frank to fill him in with the details. "Go take a picture of that tree trunk," Frank ordered. "You have to have a record of that!"

After lunch, I ventured out on my regular walk on the beach. The ocean seemed different to me this afternoon. Much like the betrayal one might feel after a caring lover suddenly became abusive, the ocean's surf I had found so calming before had shown me a sinister side. I came upon the scene of the crime and froze. The tree trunk was gone. My brush with death now hit me like a ton of bricks. The dead tree trunk had served its purpose in saving my life and had returned to the sea. A wave of such immense gratitude swept over me that I fell to my knees on the sand.

Clips of thoughts came to me in quick succession. The last time I had felt a similar surge of gratitude was after surviving the near-head-on car collision without injuries. I tried to decide which accident was more bizarre, but I couldn't. Each one was a once-in-a-lifetime event—how could two of them happen to the same person a month and a half apart? I concluded that the Universe was trying to tell me something. I walked over to a driftwood log and sat down to ponder this. For a moment I became mesmerized by the rhythm of the undulating surf. Just then a simple message rang out loud and clear: "This is not your time. You have not yet fulfilled your purpose. Keep writing what comes to your mind." Instantly any second thoughts about my writing ability dissipated. Cosmically I was being encouraged to share what I had experienced. Why should I waste another minute doubting myself when it was crystal clear that Divine Consciousness had my back? A cavalcade of material was generating in my head. I couldn't wait to get back to my computer.

10

WHERE DO WE GO FROM HERE?

What happens to our consciousness when we die? Scientists, yogis, theologians, and philosophers have been asking these questions for thousands of years. Is it the brain that creates thought, so that when one is brain-dead, consciousness ceases? Or is it the other way around—when we die, does our consciousness continue to exist?

Donald D. Hoffman, a cognitive scientist at the University of California, Irvine, examines these questions in his article “Conscious Realism and the Mind/Body Problem,” written for the journal *Mind and Matter.*

Despite substantial efforts by many researchers, we still have no scientific theory of how brain activity can create, or be, conscious experience. This is troubling since we have a large body of correlations between brain activity and consciousness, correlations normally assumed to entail that brain activity creates conscious experience. Here I explore a solution to the mind/body problem that starts with the converse assumption: these correlations arise because consciousness creates brain activity and indeed creates all objects and properties of the physical world.

In my first book, *The Divine Language of Coincidence*, I include “Appendix A: Consciousness and Quantum Mechanics.” I cite examples of experiments that, for me, give credence to the idea that consciousness permeates the Universe.

Take the phenomenon of the double-slit experiment. When particles are shot at a wall through one slit, they line up in the same position as the slit. When shot through two slits, they behave like waves, but when a measuring device is introduced, they respond as if they are conscious of being observed and turn back into particles! How is it also possible, as posited in Bell’s theorem, that particles that have been entangled in a particular way and find themselves on opposite ends of the Universe instantaneously influence each other faster than the speed of light?

One of the leading researchers into near-death experiences is Dr. Sam Parnia, director of critical care and resuscitation research at New York University's Langone Health medical center. Among his many groundbreaking studies in the past two decades, AWARE (AWAreness REsuscitation) closely examines the experiences of hundreds of patients whose brains have flatlined after cardiac arrest and before being resuscitated. The patients described lucid recollections of seeing deceased relatives and of reviewing their actions and intentions throughout their lives. Many provided detailed accounts of their resuscitation. How can people have these vivid experiences when they are brain-dead, have quit breathing, and have no pulse? Dr. Parnia is quoted in a Newsweek article: "I don't mean that people have their eyes open or that their brain is working after they die. That petrifies people. I'm saying we have a consciousness that makes up who we are—our selves, thoughts, feelings, emotions—and that entity, it seems, does not become annihilated just because we've crossed the threshold of death; it appears to keep functioning and not dissipate. How long it lingers, we can't say."

If indeed consciousness ceases when we die, how can communication with deceased people, as I have documented in these chapters, occur? So far, of all the top minds that have researched and mused about consciousness, no one has been able to provide unequivocal proof of its existence. There are findings, however, in the field of quantum mechanics that indicate it does exist.

The mystery of consciousness has prompted many serious scientists to study psi phenomena, or parapsychology, conducting experiments in telepathy, psychokinesis, and clairvoyance. Dr. Dean Radin, chief scientist at the Institute of Noetic Sciences, has been a trailblazer in parapsychology for more than four decades and has written numerous books about the subject. In *Real Magic: Ancient Wisdom, Modern Science, and a Guide to the Secret Power of the Universe* (not exactly the most scientific title), Dr. Radin gives us a guided tour from classical science to "magic" science—how astrology, alchemy, and herbalism practiced by the ancients have evolved into the modern sciences of astronomy, chemistry, and pharmaceuticals. He alludes to a future in which the quantum field of universal consciousness will offer us unlimited possibilities of psi phenomena, or real magic. By honing techniques such as meditation, affirmations, and forced will, among others, and focusing our attention/intention on a specific desired outcome, it can be manifested, Dr. Radin asserts. This claim is validated by his repeatable experimental results, as well as by a mind-boggling synchronicity that happened to him and defies the possibility that chance is a viable explanation.

Do I believe that Dr. Radin's techniques result in manifesting our desires? Absolutely, 100 percent! They work enough times for me to see that these events are not attributable to coincidence. From my own experiences, I believe that consciousness, where God resides, is real and divinely intelligent. Not only does Divine Consciousness know what is best for us much better than we do and manifests it, but it also places obstacles in our path to save us from desires that could potentially be to our detriment. This omniscience has presented me with coincidences that have resulted in miracles, as well as impediments that have kept me from harm's way. Suppose my desire is to go skydiving, but a string of obstacles occurs. I have come to accept these roadblocks as don't-do-this signs from God/Universe and have abandoned the idea. But say I decide to exercise my free will and persevere. I go skydiving; my parachute doesn't open, and I fall to my death. Unless it's for a healing, I formulate my intention by asking for what I desire followed by "or whatever is for the best." "Let go, let God" has always worked for me.

One of the many studies I found fascinating in Dr. Radin's book was unexpected—examining the role of belief. Referring to believers as sheep for their acceptance of psi phenomena, and skeptics as goats for stubbornly resisting such concepts despite empirical proof, scientists and psychologists have for decades conducted hundreds of experiments with thousands of people to determine whether belief is a factor in experiencing paranormal events and their frequency. Is it any surprise that findings show believers to report a higher level of such events than do skeptics? Even though I am a believer of unshakable faith, these findings give me an explanation of why so many miraculous events have occurred in my life. Communicating with friends and family members who have transcended earthly life has not been imagined by me or by my friends who have reported their experiences. It is inconceivable that such signs and messages can be delivered without the existence of Divine Consciousness. This is what makes me a believing sheep.

Another researcher, Masaru Emoto, believed that "water is the blueprint of our reality" and conducted experiments involving water and consciousness. He claims that words expressing emotions transmitted to water, whether with intention or written on a piece of paper and placed on a container, have a physical effect on crystals formed at a critical point in the process of being frozen. Emoto's findings show that not only positive words but also pleasant pictures and melodic music produce beautiful crystal formations, while hurtful words, ugly images, and heavy metal produce misshapen formations. One such experiment that jumped out at me began by putting rice with water in three beakers. Every day for a month, the researcher conducting it would focus his intention on the first beaker with "thank you," the second with "you idiot," and the third one by ignoring it altogether. At the end of the month, the rice in the first beaker was cheerily fermenting with clear bubbles, the second one had turned black, and the third, which had been ignored, had turned a moldy putrid green. If water is reacting to our intention, then water must be conscious. If our bodies are indeed made of up to 60 percent water and the brain and heart 73 percent, then our words and intentions must affect others.

The results of this experiment clearly illustrate that we need to be kind and encourage one another. In counseling school we learned about how emotional abuse affects children. Children who are valued and encouraged have healthy self-esteem and thrive. Those who experience emotional abuse by being told they are stupid or not good enough, or who are repeatedly ignored, often underperform, lack self-esteem, and often develop disorders that can become serious if not treated. If our intentions can physically transmute the properties of water, this has to be done through consciousness. And if that's the case, our intentions have a ripple effect that can affect the whole world.

The following experience I had during a guided meditation solidified my belief, beyond any trace of doubt, that consciousness exists and that our awareness transcends death.

Miriam would tell me stories about her mother's spiritual enlightenment and her channeling various entities, including the Virgin Mary. But it was the message Hope had channeled about our friend Joy's past life during a meditation with Miriam over the phone that had me convinced that Hope was an ascended master. When Miriam told me that Hope was coming to visit from Montana, I was eager to meet her. "I would love to meet your mother!"

After a pause Miriam replied, "Well, you know, my mother doesn't want people to know about her gift."

"I won't spill the beans," I responded. "I just want to meet her, but it's really up to you."

To my delight, Miriam called and invited me to have lunch the following Saturday with her family, including Hope. I don't know what I expected a channeler from Montana to look like, but I was surprised to be met by such a genteel, elegantly dressed lady. With her upper-crust English accent, she reminded me of Helen Mirren, the British actress. Also at lunch were Miriam's husband, their college-aged son and daughter, and her husband's parents. At the table, the conversation turned to spirituality and believers versus skeptics. Miriam's husband and father-in-law, both doctors, declared themselves atheists, and everyone weighed in for what proved to be a lively discussion. After coffee, cookies, and a delectable apple tart, Hope tilted her head toward me. "Sophia, would you like to join Miriam and me for a meditation in the study?"

I was thrilled. "Of course . . . I'd love to!" I blurted out, hardly able to believe my good fortune. I felt as if I had won a spiritual lottery. After rising, Hope led us into the den. She settled cross-legged in the notch of the L-shaped leather sofa, and Miriam and I sat at each side. Hope's face assumed an angelic look. I was completely open to whatever was going to transpire.

After having us close our eyes and guiding us with a basic relaxation exercise, Hope asked us to focus on the base of our spine, the pelvic floor, and to imagine that after entering an iron gate we were in a red garden where everything was red—the birds, the flowers, the sky, all red. She then brought our attention to just below the navel and asked us to imagine entering through another iron gate into a garden where everything was orange. At first I questioned whether the visualization was too simplistic. Recalling the gifts and abilities this woman possessed, I canceled that thought and went with the flow, immersing myself in an orange garden. I realized that Hope was guiding us through the chakras along with their corresponding colors.

Hope skipped the solar plexus chakra. She asked us to focus on our heart and imagine entering through a gate into a green garden. As soon as I visualized being in an exquisite green garden, I felt a powerful circular energetic force horizontally slicing through my heart. I had never experienced anything like it. Skipping the throat chakra, Hope brought our attention to the third eye and into a purple garden. Just as I saw myself enter the purple garden, while the energy moving through my heart chakra continued, another dynamic circuit began encircling me vertically, looping from the top of my head around my toes and up again, whoop, whoop, whoop. It was so intense that I actually wondered if I had accidentally ingested some kind of psychedelic drug.

In her soft voice, Hope guided our focus to the crown of the head, saying, "And now, as you enter through the iron gate, you find yourself in a crystalline white garden where everything is white—the flowers, the birds . . ." Entering the white garden in my mind's eye, I had a most extraordinary experience. The fierce energetic sensations I was having spontaneously ceased, and I found myself floating in space in pure light. Hope stopped talking. I became aware that I was boundless, without a body. I was one with the light! Suddenly I received a download of knowingness and thought, "Oh my God, this is where I came from, and this is where I'm going to go!"

Just then, Hope's voice changed into a deep booming voice that bellowed, "I am that I am." It was the same response that came from the burning bush after Moses called on God to help him lead the Israelites out of Egypt. The correct translation from Hebrew is "I will become whatsoever I become." In other words, God promised Moses that He would become whatever the Israelites needed Him to become—their deliverer. Through Moses, God was extending this promise to all humankind. Now, through Hope, He was reassuring us that we were supported in whatever way we needed Him to support us! I don't recall what Hope said after that, but I remember thinking at the time that the language was right out of A Course in Miracles, a channeled work through which Christ speaks to us. After Hope brought our awareness back into the room and told us to open our eyes, tears were streaming down her face as she clasped her hands together. "Oh my, I never know what to expect." I was in utter awe of Hope and what had just happened. I had been transported somewhere, but exactly where I didn't know.

My inner knowingness tells me that I had been given a sneak peek at what I am certain happens to us after we die. We remain as consciously aware as you are right now reading this. All that is shed is the body, and we become one with Divine Consciousness and the entire Universe.

IN CONCLUSION

Yes, consciousness exists beyond death. There is no ambiguity as to who had sent me the signs and messages I describe in this book, and for what reason. If I want confirmation, all I have to do is look at the timing. All of them came to me directly from the sender, except for the message I received from my father through a medium. That one contained a warning to my nephew that may have saved his life. In all cases, there was a need, and whether it was answered with advice, encouragement, confirmation, or even money, the fact that I received the messages at just the right time precludes the likelihood that they occurred by chance.

The stories of my three friends' experiences illustrate how timing was a major element in what each of them received. As Michelle and her son sat huddled together in the front seat of their car, seeking answers to what had caused the car accident that killed Heather, the speedometer needle began moving without the ignition being turned on, as if on cue, conveying to them that it was a sudden acceleration and thus providing the closure they needed.

Despite the dangerous consequences Kim would face if she was caught escaping from the labor camp run by Pol Pot's army, the urge to go home only got stronger. She risked a perilous all-night journey by foot to arrive at her family home just in time to hold her five-year-old sister before she died. By heeding her inner voice, Kim not only gave her sister her dying wish, but holding her as she died was a gift that Kim would treasure her whole life.

As Mary was mourning the death of her father, an acquaintance from her AA meeting gave her a poem her father had channeled through him, which gave her immense comfort when she needed it the most.

These are true stories of direct communication with dead loved ones who have returned to their oneness with Divine Intelligence. I have also provided accounts of experiments conducted by scientists who have devoted their lives to proving that consciousness exists. You, the reader, have to conclude whether the signs and messages that were received at just the right time were indeed communicated through consciousness . . . or if they were merely coincidences.

ACKNOWLEDGMENTS

I am literally and literarily forever indebted to my friends for inspiring five of this book's chapters. With the completion of chapter seven, I thought the book was finished. Five of the chapters were of my experiences and two, which I am so grateful for, were those of close friends, Michelle Murphy and Kim Ung. I was somewhat disappointed with the book's short word count and was secretly praying for a story from a third friend.

Then, this happened: I was having coffee with Beth

Turchi, when in the middle of the conversation she blurted out, "You are going to write about your two accidents, aren't you?"

"No, why would I do that? I didn't die, did I?"

"Precisely!" she shot back. "Those were the weirdest almost-death accidents I've ever heard. Just the fact that you survived either is beyond me." Beth had planted a seed. After the second accident involving a sneaker wave, I distinctly recalled being downloaded a message, "This is not your time. You have not yet fulfilled your purpose." I knew I had to write about the accidents.

Kathy Norris had invited me to have lunch out on her newly renovated patio. We were discussing our shared belief about how we continue to be conscious after we die. I told her about an out-of-body experience I had had during a guided meditation led by a friend's mother, who I consider to be an ascended master. During the meditation, I had suddenly found myself floating in light and, as I marveled at not having a body, I received a message, "This is where you came from and this is where you are going to go." Kathy's hand slammed down on the table, declaring, "That's how you're going to end your book!"

"But Kathy, I didn't die—the stories in the book are about communications having to do with death."

Kathy was resolute, "You experienced pure consciousness

and were told that that's where you will go when you die. This brings it back full circle to your title, Consciousness Beyond Death!" She was right and that's how the book ends.

I finally had to accept the fact that I knew all of my friends' stories and to stop hoping that I would find a third story to write about, when Mary Dutton, my best friend from Portland called. "Guess what!" she exclaimed. "I found the letter I got from my father after he died."

"What letter?"

"You know, the poem I told you about!" she insisted.

"You did not! Are you kidding Mary? You think I would forget something like you getting a poem from your father after he died? Tell me!" My prayers were answered—I had a third story to write about by none other than my best friend! Even more amazingly, the poem had been out of Mary's sight for ten years and I got it just in time to include in my book!

I also want to thank the crew at Mascot Books, my publisher, for their enthusiasm and professionalism, the support from my friends and family, and most of all, going back to my book's dedication at the beginning, I cannot overstate my gratitude to my departed friends and family that have proven to me that they are not that far away.

ABOUT THE AUTHOR

Sophia has enjoyed three diverse careers: a decade in architecture that included working with notable 20th century visionary Dr. R. Buckminster Fuller, running her own couture fashion business, and working as a mental health therapist in private practice. She also created Living a Fearless Life, a twelve-workshop program which was piloted in the Philadelphia Prison System and implemented with groups of ex-trafficked and ex-homeless women and women in recovery.

Writing books was never on Sophia's radar. She began experiencing miracles when she was nineteen. Although many people have had coincidences and serendipitous events happen to them, the prodigious number of them happening to one person is indeed remarkable. After Sophia identified the common denominator that had precipitated each miracle, she felt compelled to share her discovery and her journey in her first book, *The Divine Language of Coincidence—How Miracles Transformed My Life After I Began Paying Attention*. Since all of the miracles she had experienced were too numerous to cram into one book, her amazing coincidences and communications that had to do with death are compiled in this book. Also included are three incredible stories of contact from the dead or dying experienced by her friends.

Sophia lives a happy life with her husband, Frank, in Philadelphia, Pennsylvania.